'opulation

Sylvia M Wood

Contents

POPULATION STRUCTURE

1 The census

Look at Figure 1.1. It shows part of the *census* form used in England in early April 1981. A census has been carried out in England ever since 1801. They are usually carried out every ten years.

The aim of a census is to find out important information about the population. It is helpful to know how many children will require schooling in the years ahead, how many pensioners there are going to be, and so on. The census enables the government to see future trends and allows it to plan accordingly.

The census in England has to be completed by the **head of household** and the questions apply to those in the household on a given night. It is illegal not to complete the census.

As you can imagine, with every household completing a census, there is a huge amount of statistical information produced. This information is gathered together by the Office of Population Censuses and Surveys and processed. Nowadays all the information is stored on computers.

It is possible to obtain census information for different sized areas the smallest of which is the **enumeration district**. This is usually a few roads with a total population of about 500. Information is available for gradually larger and larger areas – **wards** (see Figure 15.7), **boroughs, counties** and **regions**.

Most geographers and **demographers** (people who study population) use census information to find out how aspects of population (like age, employment, car ownership) vary from one place to another. A useful document which gives summary information for each county is called the **County Monitor**. Your school or local library will have the Monitor for your county.

Further valuable sources of information on population are the **birth**, **death** and **marriage certificates**. Have a look at your birth certificate or that of another member of your family to see what information is recorded. Churches have **parish records** which have details of baptisms, marriages and burials (See Fig. 1.2).

Censuses are carried out in most countries of the world. However, in many developing countries they are not always very reliable for the following reasons:

1 a large number of educated people are needed to give out and collect forms;
2 people may be hostile to giving away personal information fearing taxes or military service, for example;
3 remote parts of countries can be difficult to reach;
4 the whole operation is expensive – the money might not be available.

ACTIVITIES

1 Study Figure 1.1, the 1981 census.
   a For three of the topics, suggest reasons why the information collected can be useful in planning for the future.
   b Can you suggest any other topics that should be covered in the 1991 census? Give reasons for your suggestions.
   c Although the statistics from each census are fed into a computer, names and addresses are **not**. Why do you think this is so?
   d Why is it important that all heads of household fill in the census?
   e Why do you think most censuses in Britain take place in the spring?

2 You have been asked to design the first census for a small country in the developing world. The people in the country are fairly well educated and have reasonable standards of living. However, the population is growing rapidly and the government thinks that it is about time some accurate population statistics were made available. Make up a simple census covering only those topics which you feel to be essential for future planning. Write a short introduction so that people know why the information is needed.

Figure 1.2 Parish records of deaths in London

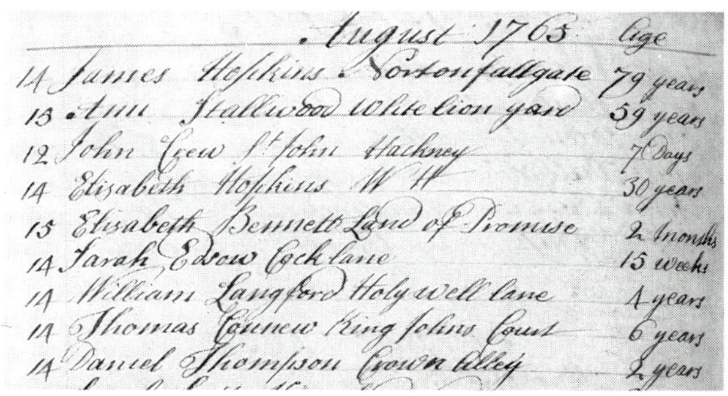
August 1763 Age
14 James Hopkins Nortonfallgate 79 years
13 Ann Stallwood White lion yard 59 years
12 John Crew St John Hackney 7 Days
14 Elisabeth Hopkins W H 30 years
15 Elisabeth Bennett Land of Promise 2 Months
14 Sarah Edrow Cocklane 15 weeks
14 William Langford Holywell lane 4 years
14 Thomas Conew King Johns Court 6 years
14 Daniel Thompson Crown Alley 2 years

Figure 1.1

In strict confidence

1981 Census England

H Form for Private Households

A household comprises **either** *one person living alone* **or** *a group of persons (who may or may not be related) living at the same address with common housekeeping. Persons staying temporarily with the household are included.*

To the Head or Joint Heads or members of the Household

Please complete this census form and have it ready to be collected by the census enumerator for your area. He or she will call for the form on **Monday 6 April 1981** or soon after. If you are not sure how to complete any of the entries on the form, the enumerator will be glad to help you when he calls. He will also need to check that you have filled in all the entries.

This census is being held in accordance with a decision made by Parliament. The leaflet headed 'Census 1981' describes why it is necessary and how the information will be used. Completion of this form is compulsory under the Census Act 1920. If you refuse to complete it, or if you give false information, you may have to pay a fine of up to £50.

Your replies will be treated in STRICT CONFIDENCE. They will be used to produce statistics but your name and address will NOT be fed into the census computer. After the census, the forms will be locked away for 100 years before they are passed to the Public Record Office.

If any member of the household who is age 16 or over does not wish you or other members of the household to see his or her personal information, then please ask the enumerator for an extra form and an envelope. The enumerator will then explain how to proceed.

When you have completed the form, please sign the declaration in Panel C on the last page.

A R THATCHER
Registrar General

Office of Population Censuses and Surveys
PO Box 200 Portsmouth PO2 8HH
Telephone 0329-42511

Please answer questions H1 - H5 about your household's accommodation, check the answer in Panel A, answer questions 1-16 overleaf and Panel B on the back page. Where boxes are provided please answer by putting a tick against the answer which applies. For example, if the answer to the marital status question is 'Single', tick box 1 thus:

1 ☑ Single

Please use ink or ballpoint pen.

To be completed by the Enumerator

Census District	Enumeration District	Form Number

Name ....

Address ....

....

.... Postcode ☐☐☐☐☐☐☐

Panel A
To be completed by the Enumerator and amended, if necessary, by the person(s) signing this form.

This household's accommodation is:

- In a caravan ☐ 20
- In any other mobile or temporary structure ☐ 30
- In a purpose-built block of flats or maisonettes ☐ 12
- In any other permanent building in which the entrance from **outside** the building is:
  - NOT SHARED with another household ☐ 10
  - SHARED with another household ☐ 11

H1 Rooms

Please count the rooms in your household's accommodation.

Do not count:

small kitchens, that is those under 2 metres (6ft 6ins) wide, bathrooms, WCs.

Number of rooms ....

Note
Rooms divided by curtains or portable screens count as one; those divided by a fixed or sliding partition count as two.

Rooms used solely for business, professional or trade purposes should be excluded.

H2 Tenure

How do you and your household occupy your accommodation? Please tick the appropriate box.

As an owner occupier (including purchase by mortgage):

1 ☐ of freehold property
2 ☐ of leasehold property

By renting, rent free or by lease:

3 ☐ from a local authority (council or New Town)
4 ☐ with a job, shop, farm or other business
5 ☐ from a housing association or charitable trust
6 ☐ furnished from a private landlord, company or other organisation
7 ☐ unfurnished from a private landlord, company or other organisation

In some other way:

☐ Please give details

....

Note
a If the accommodation is occupied by lease originally granted for, or since extended to, more than 21 years, tick box 2.
b If a share in the property is being bought under an arrangement with a local authority, New Town corporation or housing association, *for example, shared ownership (equity sharing), a co-ownership scheme,* tick box 1 or 2 as appropriate.

H3 Amenities

Has your household the use of the following amenities on these premises? Please tick the appropriate boxes.

- A fixed bath or shower permanently connected to a water supply and a waste pipe

1 ☐ YES – for use only by this household
2 ☐ YES – for use also by another household
3 ☐ NO fixed bath or shower

- A flush toilet (WC) with entrance inside the building

1 ☐ YES – for use only by this household
2 ☐ YES – for use also by another household
3 ☐ NO inside flush toilet (WC)

- A flush toilet (WC) with entrance outside the building

1 ☐ YES – for use only by this household
2 ☐ YES – for use also by another household
3 ☐ NO outside flush toilet (WC)

H4
Please answer this question if box 11 in Panel A is ticked.

Are your rooms (not counting a bathroom or WC) enclosed behind your own front door **inside** the building?

1 ☐ YES   2 ☐ NO

If your household has only one room (not including a bathroom or WC) please answer 'YES'.

H5 Cars and vans

Please tick the appropriate box to indicate the number of cars and vans normally available for use by you or members of your household (other than visitors).

0 ☐ None
1 ☐ One
2 ☐ Two
3 ☐ Three or more

Include any car or van provided by employers if normally available for use by you or members of your household but **exclude** vans used solely for the carriage of goods.

2 Population pyramids

A **population pyramid**, sometimes called an age-sex graph, uses horizontal bars to represent the proportion of people of either sex in different age groups. Put together, the bars often form a diagram that looks like a pyramid, hence the name. Figure 2.1 shows population pyramids for England and Wales in 1901 and 1981. Which one looks most like a pyramid?

Population pyramids tell us a lot about the population structure and aid planning. A number of typical shapes can be identified – see Figure 2.2.

True pyramidal shaped diagrams (Figure 2.2a) tell us that the population has a lot of young people but few elderly. Birth rates would be high as would death rates with few people living to old age. Such pyramid shapes are typical of developing countries where populations are **expanding**.

The graph in Figure 2.2b shows a fairly **stationary** population with fewer children and most of the population aged between fifteen and sixty years old. Figure 2.2c shows a **contracting** population where the birth rate is steadily dropping year by year and where there are a lot of elderly people. Both Figures 2.2b and 2.2c are common shapes for countries in the developed world.

The study of population pyramids is helpful for future planning. A 'baby boom' can be identified and then catered for accordingly as the 'boom' moves up the diagram over the years through childhood, to adulthood and into old age.

The following activities will further your understanding of population pyramids.

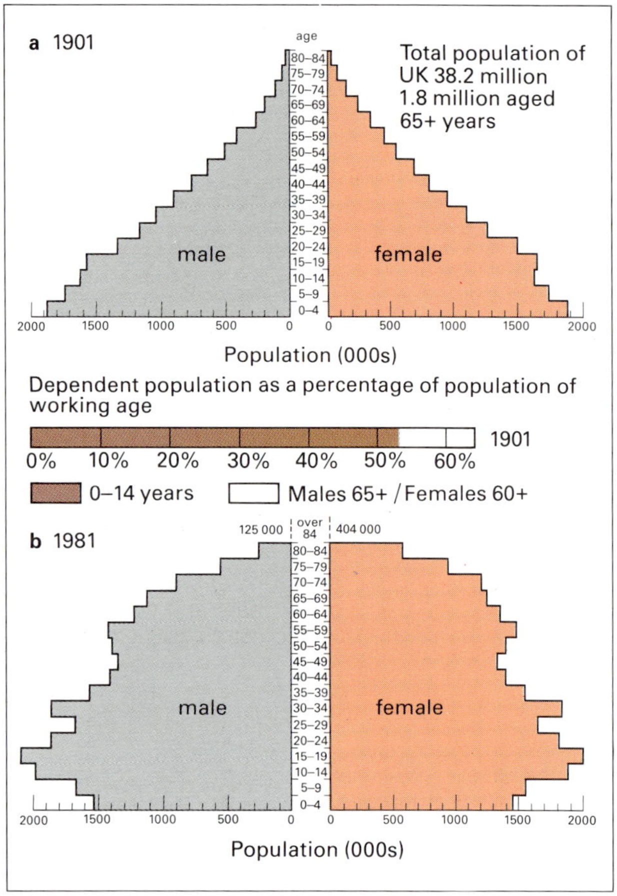

Figure 2.1 The age and sex structure of the population of England and Wales in 1901 and 1981. For 1981 the populations, male and female, over 84 years old are shown as numbers.

Figure 2.2 Population pyramids.

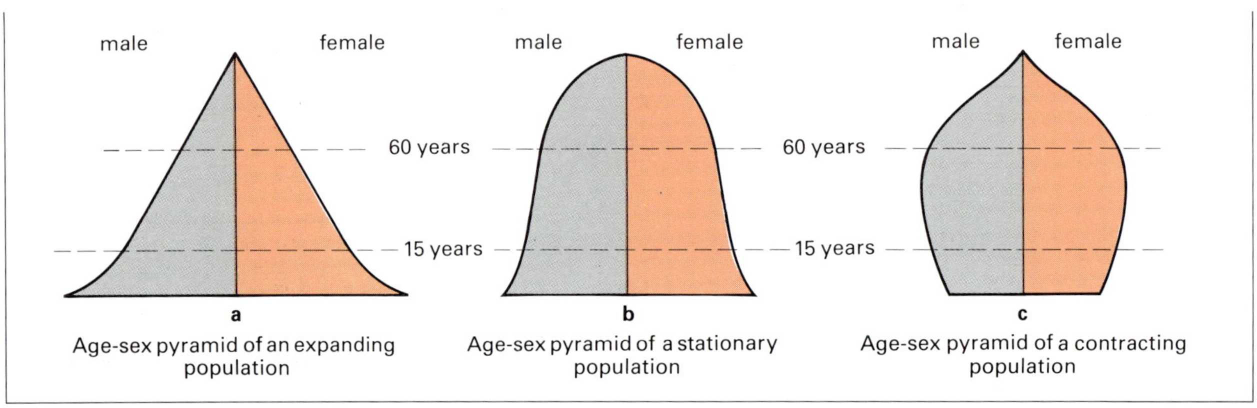

ACTIVITIES

1 a Make a copy of each of the pyramid shapes in Figure 2.2. Give each a title. Use three different colours to shade the sections 1–15 years, 15–60 years and over 60 years. Do this for each pyramid.

b Which pyramid has the highest proportion of under 15s?

c Which pyramid has the lowest proportion of under 15s?

d In twenty years time, which pyramid will suggest a need to provide for the greatest proportion of elderly?

2 Study Figure 2.1.

a For each pyramid, use Figure 2.2 to state whether the population is **expanding**, **stationary** or **contracting**.

b Use both graphs to contrast the female population (thousands) in the following age groups:
 i 0–4 age group;
 ii 30–34 age group;
 iii 75–79 age group.

c Suggest reasons for the changing trends you have identified.

d Study Figure 2.1b. Explain why school closures are likely in the next few years and why the Government must plan to set aside more money for pensions.

e Make a tracing of the outline of Figure 2.1b. Give it a title and add the following labels:
 i large proportion of elderly;
 ii decreasing proportion of infants;
 iii effect of the Second World War;
 iv effect of the 1960s 'baby boom'.
 Be careful with the last two labels!

3 a Use the information in Table 2.1 to draw a population pyramid for England and Wales in 1986. Give the diagram a title.

b Comment on the changing trends between 1981 (Figure 2.1b) and 1986. Do you think these trends will continue into the first part of the 21st century?

4 a Trace the population pyramid for Nigeria from Figure 2.3a. Use the same three colours used in Activity **1a** to shade the three age groups 0–15, 15–60 and 60+. Add labels to highlight the contrasts with the 1986 pyramid for England and Wales drawn in Activity **3**.

b Is this an **expanding**, **stationary** or **contracting** population?

c What planning guidelines for the next ten years would you give the Government?

d Repeat exercises **a**, **b** and **c** for West Germany using Figure 2.3b.

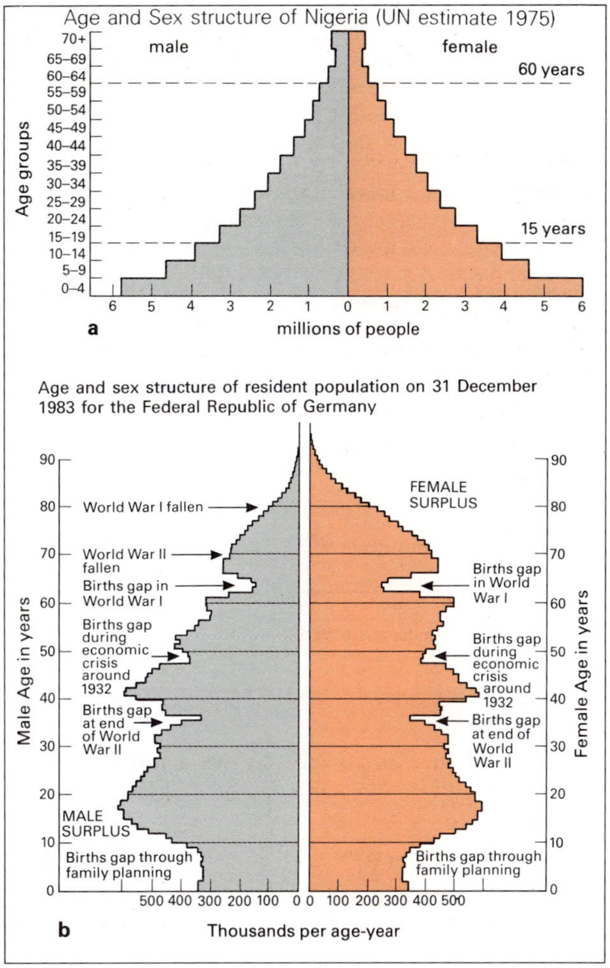

Figure 2.3

Table 2.1 Estimated resident population of England and Wales in mid 1986 in thousands

Age in years	Males	Females
0–4	1632.2	1551.0
5–9	1553.3	1471.3
10–14	1651.9	1561.6
15–19	2004.5	1906.7
20–24	2130.4	2072.2
25–29	1877.0	1847.0
30–34	1683.0	1658.3
35–39	1851.2	1848.7
40–44	1593.2	1570.1
45–49	1394.2	1382.0
50–54	1334.0	1332.7
55–59	1328.9	1374.0
60–64	1299.4	1415.1
65–69	1071.5	1279.3
70–74	897.2	1210.1
75–79	625.9	1014.0
80–84	325.9	688.6
85–89	113.6	343.1
Over 90	36.3	145.9

Source: OPCS Monitor

ACTIVITIES

5 People below 15 and over 60 are sometimes referred to as **dependants**. They are generally looked after by those people aged 15–60. Work out the percentage of dependants for England and Wales from Table 2.1. To do this, add up the number of people below fifteen and over sixty. Divide this by the **total** population and multiply by 100.

Comment on any differences between the percentage of young and old dependants in 1901 (from Figure 2.1a) and your results for 1986. (See Figs. 2.4 and 2.5.)

6 Population pyramids can be drawn for towns. These often reveal interesting patterns.

a Use the information in Tables 2.2 and 2.3 to draw pyramids for Eastbourne and Stevenage 'New Town'.

b Use labels to compare the two graphs.

c Try to explain any differences.

Figure 2.4 An English family in 1901

Table 2.2 Eastbourne's population 1981 census

Age in years	Males	Females
0–4	1712	1600
5–9	1822	1783
10–14	2147	2091
15–19	2293	2460
20–24	2120	2274
25–29	1857	2017
30–34	2226	2312
35–39	1849	1895
40–44	1595	1731
45–49	1589	1768
50–54	1714	2126
55–59	1843	2472
60–64	1992	2728
65–69	2392	3477
70–74	2346	3688
75–79	1698	3184
80–84	923	2238
85+	495	1641
Total	32 613	41 485

Total population of Eastbourne 74 098

Age in years	Total number of people	Percentage of the population
0–14	7731	10.4%
15–59	39 565	53.4%
Over 60	26 802	36.2%

Source: OPCS 1981 Census – small area statistics

Figure 2.5 An English family in the 1980s

Table 2.3 Population of Stevenage 1981

Age	Male	%	Female	%
0–4	2577	7.01	2409	6.38
5–15	6647	18.07	6380	16.91
16–24	6498	17.67	6345	16.82
25–34	6020	16.37	5681	15.01
35–44	4340	11.80	4627	12.26
45–54	4316	11.73	4522	11.99
55–59	2127	5.78	1960	5.19
60–64	1453	3.95	1557	4.13
65–69	1191	3.24	1356	3.59
70–74	837	2.28	1191	3.16
75+	777	2.11	1712	4.54
Total	36 783		37 730	

Source: Stevenage Urban Studies Centre

Figure 2.6 Retirement in Eastbourne

ACTIVITIES

7 Study Figure 2.7 which shows the distribution of people aged over sixty-five in the UK in 1981.

a Which counties had over nineteen per cent of their population made up of elderly people?

b Try to explain the pattern shown in Figure 2.7. Climate maps might help! Look in national newspapers for house prices in different areas of the country.

Figure 2.7 The elderly population of the UK in 1981

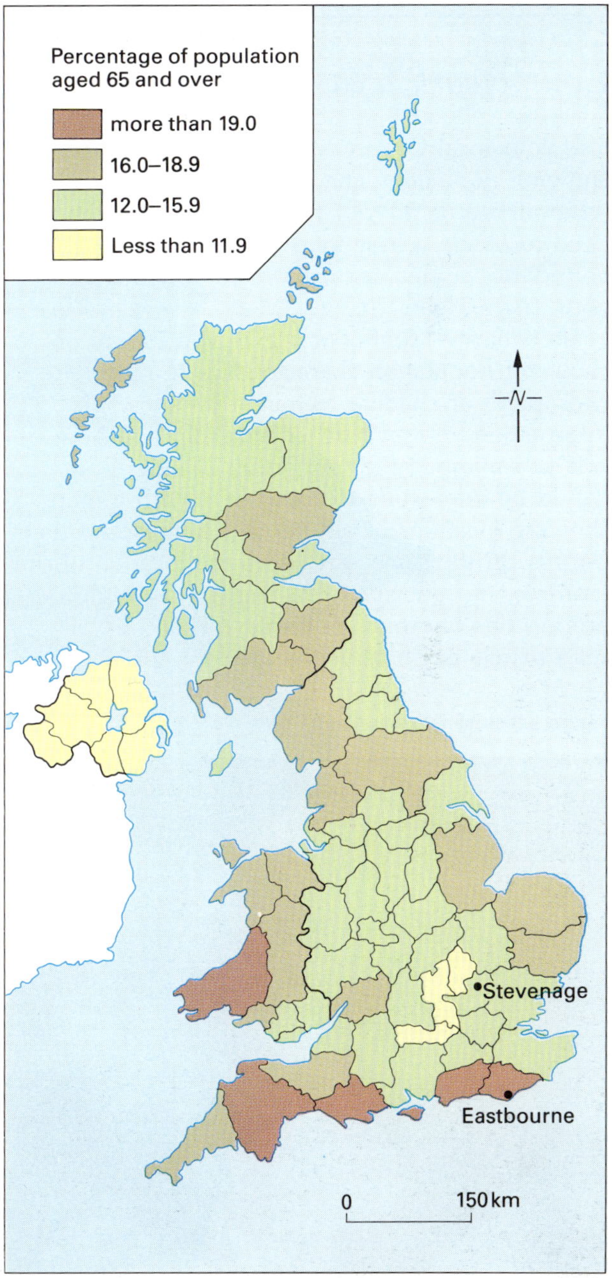

ACTIVITIES

8 Trace the triangular graph in Figure 2.8. Plot on it the position of Stevenage according to its population structure. In what way does its position differ from Eastbourne's?

9 Study the information in Table 2.4. It describes the age distribution of population in the UK by ethnic group. For each ethnic group draw a pie chart or divided bar to show the age distribution. On each diagram, use the same colour to represent each of the five age groups. (See Fig. 2.9.)
Describe the main differences and try to suggest some reasons for them.

Table 2.4 Age distribution by ethnic groups in the United Kingdom for 1983–85 combined. Percentages of ethnic groups

Age	White	West Indian	Indian	Pakistani or Bangladeshi	Other
0–15 years	22	27	34	48	37
16–24 years	14	23	15	13	18
25–44 years	27	26	33	24	32
45–64 years	22	21	14	13	10
65+ years	15	3	4	2	3

Source: OPCS Monitor GH5 86/1, 1986

Figure 2.8 Triangular graph showing population structure in 1981

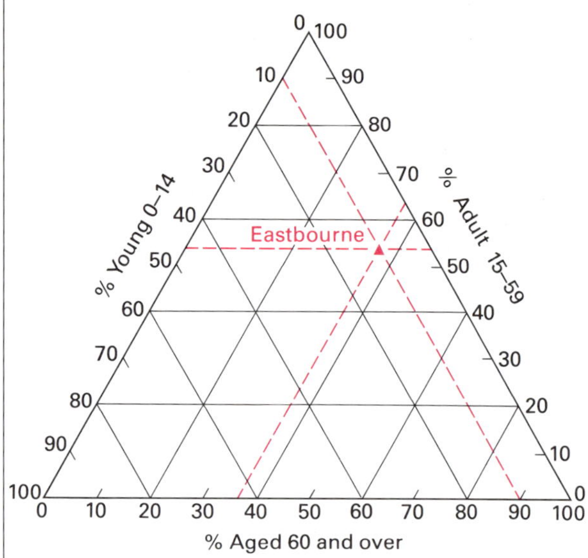

Coursework ideas

Use your local County Monitor to produce maps showing population characteristics for the different wards in your town. To do this you will need to obtain a base map showing the ward boundaries – this can usually be obtained from your Town Hall.

The County Monitor will give you plenty of choice of population characteristics to map. Use a **choropleth** or shading technique to show the information – your teacher will help you here.

If you mapped the proportion of elderly, it would be interesting to compare it with a map showing locations of old peoples homes and day centres. In the same way, does the location of, for example, mosques occur in wards with high proportions of ethnic minorities? There are all sorts of relationships you could look for.

Figure 2.9 British youth

3 Introduction to population change

The cartoon in Figure 3.1 shows how the number of people in an area or country changes.

All the time babies are born and people are dying. On average 3.9 children are born to each woman in the world. Sometimes during a war fewer children are born as families may be separated or people may not choose to have children at such dangerous times. During famines the number of births may fall as mothers may be ill-nourished. If women decide they want an education or a career they may decide to put-off having children. Sometimes people decide they do not want any children. In all these cases the **crude birth-rate** may be low.

Large numbers of births occur when people do not want or do not know how to prevent pregnancy. Read the story of Mamtaz in Figure 3.2

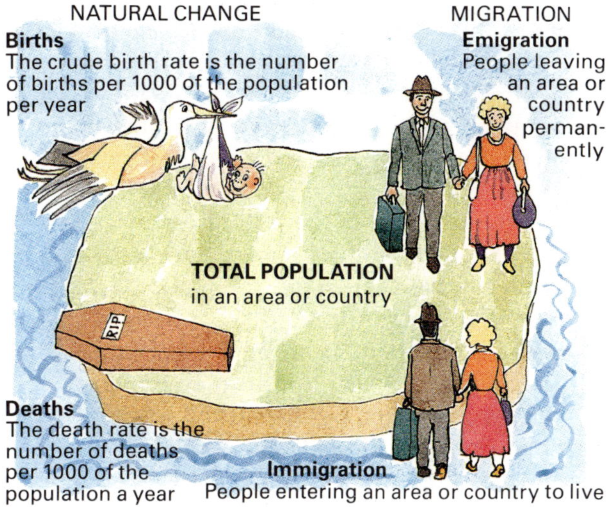

Figure 3.1 Components of population change

Figure 3.2

Mamtaz

Mamtaz is a small, very pretty woman in her early twenties. She lives in a typically poor, inaccessible, Bangladeshi village at Kaligonj, to the north of Dhaka. She was married at 13, and has had six children.

"My father's village is Dara Bakyti, about five miles from here. He was a farmer and I was the only daughter born to my mother: my stepmother had three.

I was married at 13 and had my first child when I was 14. I had no problems because my mother-in-law looked after him. It was an easy birth, after eight months, and he was very well.

Two years later I had a second boy, but he died after seven days from tetanus infection. My fifth child also died. My youngest daughter is three.

I did not use family planning because we did not have any facilities here. Recently I have tried Pills, but have had headaches. I also tried an IUD but I had problems with that. I don't want any more children but I don't know what to do.

Now I can look back and think what harm my parents did in getting me married so soon. If they had educated me maybe I would be in a better position now. My husband's income is not enough to maintain the family.

If I cannot afford to educate our two daughters, and have to get them married early, their position will be just like mine."

and see Fig. 3.3. In countries with no welfare provision for the elderly and few interests possible outside the home, people may need a large number of children for support and comfort. Look at Figure 3.4 which shows the reasons people give for having children. Some people like large families or belong to a religion like Roman Catholicism which forbids contraception. In these examples the crude birth-rate may be high.

Deaths may occur through old age, disease or accident. Through a natural or man-made hazard like famine or war, the number of deaths rises.

The relationship between the birth-rate and **death-rate** is constantly changing but the difference is known as the **natural increase or natural change**. Table 3.1 shows how birth and death rates have changed in the United Kingdom this century.

Of course variations in birth and death rates are not the only factors which explain population change. **Migration** or movements of people also help explain population losses or gains. **Immigrants** into an area to live increase numbers (see Fig. 3.5) and **emigrants** leaving an area or country permanently may reduce numbers.

Table 3.1 Birth and death rates and life expectancy in the UK

Year	Crude birth rate per 1000	Death rate per 1000	Average life expectancy
1901	30	17	Less than 55 years
1981	13	12	74 years

Source: OPCS

Figure 3.3 Mamtaz

Figure 3.4 Reasons for having children.

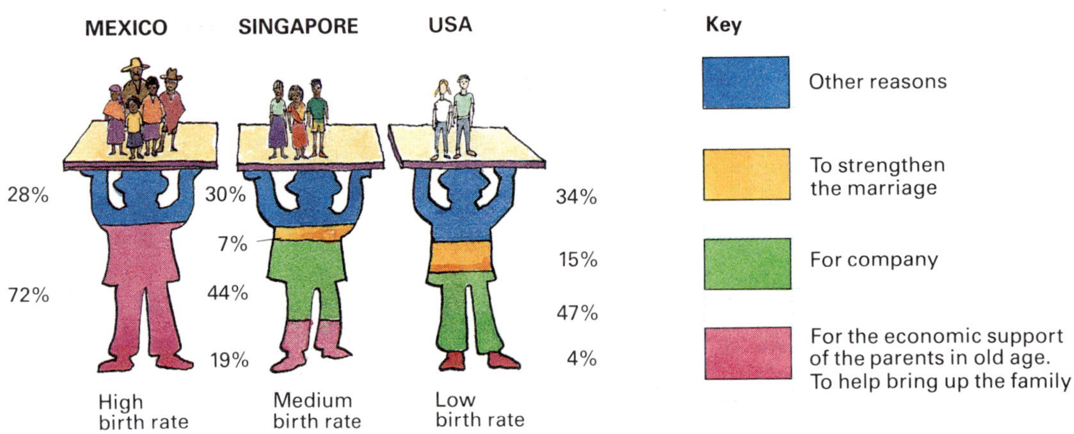

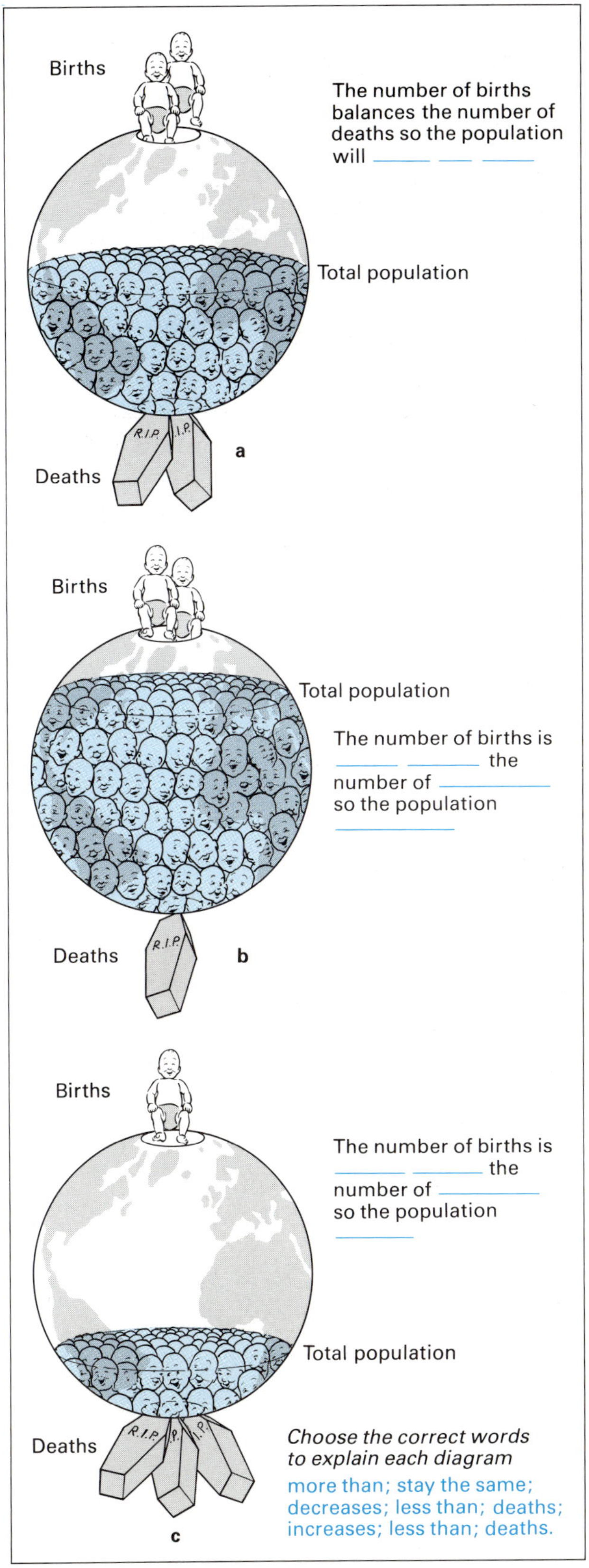

Figure 3.6 Natural population changes

Figure 3.5 Immigrants to the USA last century

ACTIVITIES

1 Copy the diagram from Figure 3.1 showing how population in an area changes.

2 a Trace or copy Figure 3.6.

  b Complete the captions by each diagram. (Migration may also be important.)

  c Add labels to each diagram of reasons why the number of births may be high; the number of deaths may be high; the number of births may be low; the number of deaths may be low.

3 Work out the natural increase – the difference between the birth-rate and death-rate in the United Kingdom in 1901 and 1981 from Table 3.1.

4 Look at Figure 3.4. Describe in what ways the reasons for having children differ in Mexico, Singapore and the USA.

4 Global population change

Read the newspaper extract in Figure 4.2. It reports that in the summer of 1987 world population probably reached five billion people or 5 000 000 000. It has risen by 3 000 000 000 in only about sixty years!

Geographers are interested in the rate at which world population is growing and the location of the increases.

For centuries population did not increase very much. Death rates were high through food shortages and disease. People did not live very long. Their **life expectancy** – or the likely length of time on average a person could expect to live – was short. Notice in Table 3.1 that even in 1901 in the United Kingdom on average people could only expect to live fifty-five years.

However, through discoveries in medicine, curing and preventing diseases like smallpox and tuberculosis, people are living longer. Better hygiene and housing and diets for many have also caused the death-rate to fall in many parts of the World. Notice that Table 4.1 shows life expectancy is over seventy years of age for most people in developed countries.

Although many people have a comparatively short life in developing countries – it is on average only just over forty years in several African countries – many children are born and survive into adulthood (see Fig. 4.1).

Study Figure 4.3 which shows where the greatest rates of population growth occur. Compare the areas with the values in Tables 4.1 and 4.2. Every country with a population growth of three per cent or more a year can expect to double its population in twenty-four years!

Table 4.2 The rates at which population doubles

Percentage natural increase in population	Doubling time in years
1	70
2	35
3	24
4	17

Figure 4.1 Village life with many children, Nigeria

My five billionth baby

EARLIER this summer I was invited to a solemn celebration — a special United Nations conference to mark the imminent birth of the five billionth inhabitant of the planet.

The first 'billion baby' did not arrive until around the beginning of the last century — three million years or so after humans appeared on earth.

The second 'billion baby' arrived sometime in the 1920s, the third about 1958, the fourth in 1975. The acceleration is staggering. Four of the five 'billion babies' are probably still alive.

Demographers hope that the pace of increase will slow after that, but they do not expect world population to stabilise until it has reached 10 billion — double what it is today.

The greatest increases will be in the Third World, and the greatest strains, as ever, upon the world's poorest people.

Already three quarters of humanity live in the Third World, and 95 per cent of future growth will occur there. And the most rapid growth of all is in the poorest developing countries, particularly in Africa, which will become the second most populous continent.

In 1950 Africa's population was half the size of Europe's; before 2050 it will be three times as great. Kenya's population is doubling every 17 years; Nigeria is expected to become the world's most populous nation after China and India.

So the burden piles up intolerably on the weakest shoulders. If the five billionth baby has been born in Africa in 1987 it is nearly 20 times more likely to die before its first birthday in Sierra Leone, for example, than in Britain. It can expect to live to the grand old age of 34.

Even now only half the children in the world's poorest countries (mostly in sub-Saharan Africa) complete primary school; fewer than a quarter of the boys — fewer than a tenth of girls — even start secondary education. Only a quarter can get safe drinking water; less have any form of sanitation.

Trying to improve these woeful statistics would be hard enough, given the chronic poverty of the continent, even if the problem remained the same size. But the problem is doubling every 25 years along with the population.

As it is, enormous achievements have already been destroyed. Since independence, Africa has increased food production faster than Europe and the United States. But population has grown so fast that each African has a fifth less food to eat.

On the one side, there are those — who say that population growth is neutral, or even beneficial, in its effects and that nothing should be done. The United States and other countries are already reducing their support for population control.

On the other hand, there are those who attribute virtually all the world's problems to population growth.

To the rest of us, population growth is highly destructive, but it is neither the root of the world's problems, nor could it be simply controlled. It is a highly complicated social and economic issue.

In the seventh-century both birth rates and death rates were high — as for most of human history. Then health and sanitation improved in Europe in the nineteenth century, death rates fell, and population soared. Our great-grandparents did not start breeding like rabbits, but they did stop dying like flies. As they got richer people had fewer children, and population stabilised.

The same 'demographic transition' has begun, much more savagely, in the Third World. Death rates dropped from the 1950s, as life expectancy grew, and diseases like cholera, smallpox and typhus were beaten back. But birth rates are only beginning to turn down.

Medical technology provided death-control, so it was natural to look to it for birth control. But many early contraceptive programmes in the Third World proved disappointing — because people *wanted* lots of children.

They want them for good reasons. From the age of 10, children often produce more for the family by work in the fields than they consume. They provide security in old age. And infant mortality is still so high that an Indian couple needs to have more than six children to be statistically sure of having one surviving son.

As people become a little less poor and more secure, their desire for large families generally falls. And as women receive more education, better opportunities, and more rights the birth rate falls even faster.

At the same time, surveys have shown that many women would have fewer children if they could get effective contraception. So the best hope is by both providing the technology, and by fighting poverty. Where the two have gone hand in hand there have been astonishing successes. But attempts to short-circuit the process by compulsory sterilisation, as in Mrs Gandhi's India, have ended in disaster.

Providing the contraceptives is relatively easy. Fighting poverty is extraordinarily difficult, for it involves changing entrenched economic and political relationships both between and within countries.

Yet it must be done, not just to defuse the population bomb, but to address the appalling conditions of the billion poorest people already on earth, and to relieve the threats to farmland and forest, which are caused as much by poverty as by population growth.

Geoffrey Lean *Obsever* 5.7.87

Figure 4.2

Table 4.1 Population totals: growth rates: life expectancy and Gross National Product for selected countries in 1985

Country	Population in millions	Percentage population growth rate 1973–1986	Life expectancy	GNP per capita in US$
*Algeria	21.9	3.1	60	2570
*Argentina	30.5	1.6	70	2120
*Australia	15.8	1.3	76	12370
*Austria	7.5	0.0	74	9100
*Bangladesh	100.6	2.5	51	150
Belgium	9.9	0.1	75	8320
*Bolivia	6.4	2.7	53	490
Botswana	1.1	4.2	57	810
Brazil	135.5	2.3	65	1660
Brunei	0.2	3.7	74	16890
*Burkina Faso	7.9	2.3	45	150
*Canada	25.4	1.2	76	14040
Chile	12.0	1.7	70	1440
*China	1041.0	1.4	69	320
*Colombia	28.4	1.9	65	1320
Denmark	5.1	0.1	75	11280
*Ecuador	9.4	2.9	66	1160
Egypt	48.5	2.7	61	660
*Ethiopia	42.2	2.6	45	110
France	55.1	0.5	78	9760
Gambia	0.7	3.5	41	230
German Dem. Rep. (East Germany)	16.7	−0.1	71	na
*German Fed. Rep. (West Germany)	61.0	−0.1	75	11040
*Ghana	12.7	2.7	53	370
Greece	9.9	0.9	72	3610
Guinea-Bissau	0.9	3.5	39	180
Hong Kong	5.4	2.3	76	6120
India	765.1	2.2	56	270
*Indonesia	162.2	2.2	55	530
Ireland	3.6	1.0	74	4770
Israel	4.3	2.1	75	6220
Italy	57.1	0.3	77	7700
Ivory Coast	10.0	4.3	53	650
Jamaica	2.2	1.2	73	910
*Japan	120.7	0.8	77	11270
*Kenya	20.4	4.0	54	290
Kuwait	1.7	5.5	72	14870
*Libya	3.7	4.3	60	7170
Luxembourg	0.4	0.2	74	14300
*Malawi	7.0	3.1	45	170
*Malaysia	15.6	2.4	68	1980
*Mexico	78.8	2.8	67	2100
*Netherlands	14.5	0.6	77	9380
*Nigeria	99.7	2.9	50	820
Norway	4.1	0.4	77	14510
*Pakistan	96.1	3.1	51	340
*Portugal	10.2	1.0	74	1960
Romania	22.7	0.7	72	na
*Saudi Arabia	11.5	4.8	62	8620
Singapore	2.6	1.3	73	7590
South Africa	32.4	2.4	55	2030
Spain	38.6	0.9	77	4280
*Switzerland	6.4	0.1	77	16330
Tanzania	22.2	3.4	52	280
*Trinidad and Tobago	1.2	1.6	69	6100
United Kingdom	56.5	0.0	75	8430
*United States	239.2	1.0	76	16730
USSR	277.4	0.9	70	na
*Venezuela	17.3	3.2	70	3080
Zambia	6.7	3.3	52	410

Source: World Bank Atlas 1987 and 1988 update.

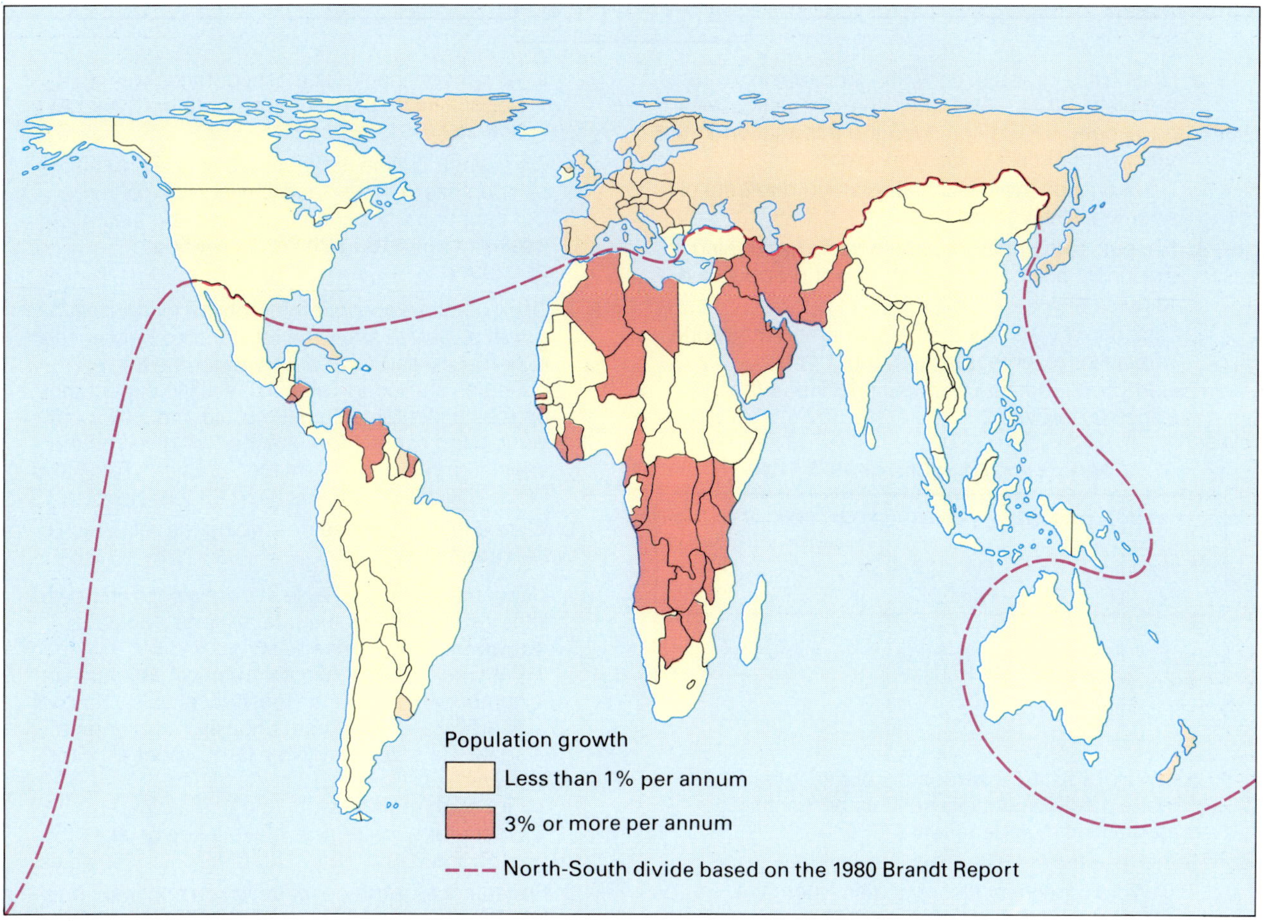

Figure 4.3 The world divided into the richer 'North' and poorer 'South', showing areas of population growth. (Arno Peters Projection)

As you can see from the map in Figure 4.3 and Table 4.1 the countries with the fastest rates of population growth are some of the poorest. In many cases their GNP is under US $1000 per person a year. (**Gross National Product** (GNP) means the total value of all goods and services produced in a country in a year, divided by the total population.)

Countries like The Gambia, Malawi, and elsewhere in Africa in particular are very poor and are finding it hard to develop and improve their economies.

Population growth rates are much lower in many developed, richer countries.

Table 4.3 Estimates of world population growth by region (in millions)

Year	Europe and the USSR	Asia	Africa	Latin America	North America	Oceania
1750	167	498	106	16	2	2
1800	208	630	107	24	7	2
1850	284	801	111	38	26	2
1900	430	925	133	74	82	6
1950	572	1381	222	162	166	13
Estimate 2000	880	3458	768	638	354	32

ACTIVITIES

1 a Draw a line-graph to show the increase in world population from 1650 when the population may have been 500 million. Use the information in the article in Figure 4.2 for your graph.
Put time on the horizontal axis and numbers of people on the vertical axis.
b Beneath the graph describe what is happening to the length of time it is taking for world population to double itself.
c Discuss why you should be concerned that world population is increasing at a rapid rate.

2 Divide your paper into five columns. Head the columns as follows:

Areas of Population Change 1973–1985

Population loss	Population growth of 0 to 1% per annum	Population growth of +1% to 2% per annum	Population growth of +2% to 3% per annum	Population growth of +3% per annum

a Using Table 4.1 insert each country into its correct column according to its percentage population change recently.
b Look up the location of all the countries listed.
i Which continent has countries where the population is not increasing?
ii Which continent has most countries with a population increase of over three per cent per annum?
c On a world outline of Figure 4.3 shade and name all countries with a population increase of three per cent or more per annum. Describe their position compared with the 'North-South' boundary.

3 a Draw a scattergraph, preferably on log/normal graph paper, to show the relationship between life expectancy and GNP per head for the thirty countries starred in Table 4.1. Put life expectancy on the horizontal, arithmetic scale and GNP on the vertical log scale. (Your teacher will give you the special graph paper from the *Teacher's Book* and discuss with you why it is used for this exercise.)
b Write a few sentences describing the relationship the graph shows.

4 a Using the figures in Table 4.3 draw superimposed line graphs to show the rate of world population growth by region since 1750.
i Put time on the horizontal axis and estimates of numbers of people on the vertical axis. (You will need to take great care choosing your vertical scale. Be sure you have a large sheet of graph paper!)
ii Plot each region in turn and use a different colour for each region. Make a key or label each line.
b Beneath the graph describe which continent has had the fastest rate of growth this century and which the slowest.

5 National population change

In Britain we do not know for sure what the population size was before 1801. In that year the first census gave the total as 10.5 million. Table 5.1 shows the growth of population in the United Kingdom this century.

Look at Figure 5.1. It shows how population grew mainly through natural increase rather than immigration. The death rate fell from about seventeen per 1000 in 1901 to twelve per 1000 in 1981. Better diet, clean drinking water and health care helped reduce the number of deaths. In 1868 an Act of Parliament allowed bad houses to be condemned as unfit for people to live in (see Fig. 5.2). Medical Officers and Health and Sanitary Inspectors were established after an Act in 1875. Both these Acts improved conditions especially for poor working people.

If you talk to your grandparents or elderly friends, they will probably tell you that they were from a big family with several brothers and sisters. As children survived, the birth rate slowed down. Look at Figure 3.1 which shows this. Family size in England and Wales has fallen so that on average there are now about two children per family (see Figs. 2.4 and 2.5). In countries like West Germany less than two children are born in each family on average.

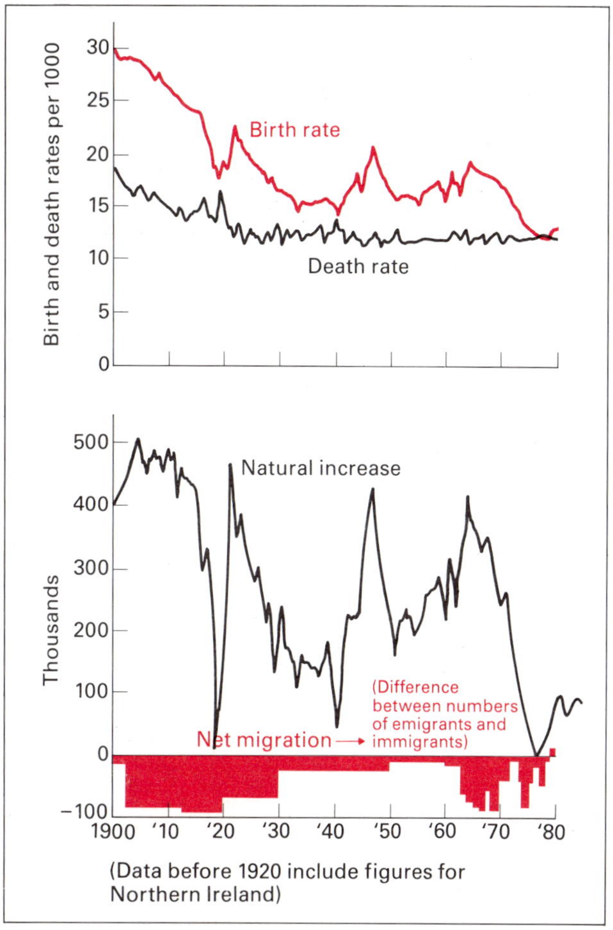

Figure 5.1 Factors affecting population growth in the UK.

Figure 5.2 Unhealthy conditions in nineteenth century Britain

Table 5.1 Population of the United Kingdom

Year	Totals in thousands
1901	38237
1911	42082
1921	44027
1931	46038
1941	No census during World War II
1951	50290
1961	52807
1971	55928
1981	56352

Source: OPCS

Table 5.2 China's changing population

Year	Population total to nearest million	Birth rate per 1000	Death rate per 1000
1953	588	37	14.0
1964	695	39	11.5
1981	997	21	6.4

Figure 5.3 English counties showing the greatest change of population (projections 1983–1991).

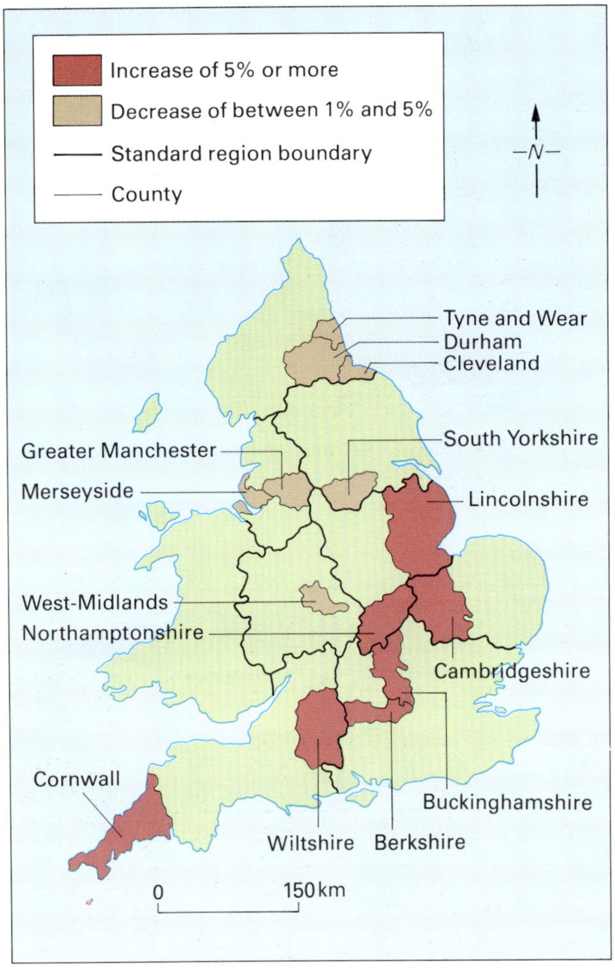

Of course population rates of change vary in different parts of a country. Figure 5.3 shows that, in Britain, counties like Berkshire and Cornwall have increasing populations. People are moving to areas where there is work and an attractive environment (see Fig. 5.4). Declining industrial areas like Cleveland and Merseyside are losing population.

Look at Table 5.2. China is the country with the largest population in the world. It has about 1000 million people. It had a population of about 542 million in 1949 when the Communists came to power. With high birth rates and falling death rates its population continues to grow (see Fig. 5.5) in spite of famine in some years.

In Nigeria, as in many developing countries, population is growing rapidly through very high birth rates – possibly seventy-four per 1000 in places. In eastern Nigeria the average age of marriage is 15. There is little use of contraception and more than eight children in a family is common in rural areas.

People in towns in African and Latin American countries have access to family planning clinics and education (see Fig. 5.6). Look at Table 5.3. These people tend to have fewer children than those in rural areas. In many Asian countries birth rates are high in towns and the countryside.

Figure 5.4 New homes in Milton Keynes, Buckinghamshire

Table 5.3 Urban and rural fertility for selected countries

Country	Average for continent	Average number of children per family for a five year period in the 1970s	
		Urban	Rural
Kenya		1.00	1.44
Ghana		1.02	1.11
	Africa	1.03	1.17
Mexico		1.17	1.29
Venezuela		1.00	1.50
	Latin America	0.96	1.19
Bangladesh		1.08	0.98
Indonesia		0.77	0.83
Malaysia		0.88	1.02
Fiji		0.80	0.93
	Asia and Oceania	1.04	1.05

Table 5.4 Average annual population growth rates in percentages in urban and rural areas of selected countries

Country	% Urban population	Average annual growth in % 1975–1980	
		Urban	Rural
Bangladesh	11.2	6.7	2.4
Brazil	67.0	4.0	−0.5
Egypt	45.4	3.4	1.9
Ethiopia	14.5	6.1	1.2
Indonesia	20.2	3.6	1.3
Kenya	14.2	7.3	3.5
Mexico	66.7	4.1	0.9
Venezuela	88.3	4.3	0.1

Figure 5.5 Some of China's people

Figure 5.6 A family planning clinic in a Nigerian town

ACTIVITIES

1 a Draw a line graph using information in Table 5.1 to show population change in the United Kingdom this century. Put time on the horizontal or x axis and population on the vertical or y axis.
Give the graph a heading.

b Comment on the trend and rate of change of the United Kingdom's population this century.

2 a Work out the natural increase – the difference between the birth rate and death rate – in the United Kingdom in 1901 and 1981 from Table 3.1.

b Why did the United Kingdom's population increase rapidly in the early part of the twentieth century?

c Interview and record a talk with an elderly person about what their home life was like when they were a child.
i Try to find out whether they were part of a large or small family.
ii Compare their memories with your family life today. You could produce a written or tape-recorded report of your investigations.

3 a Draw four proportional circles to show China's population in 1949, 1953, 1964 and 1981 from Table 5.2 and figures in the text. Use the square root of the population at each date to work out the radius of your circles. For example:

1949 $\sqrt{(542 \text{ million})} = 23.3$ million

Therefore 23.3 mm. will be the radius of your circle representing China's population in 1949.
Keep the same scale of 1 mm to 1 unit for each circle so they are comparable. Label each diagram.

b Describe what has happened to China's population since 1949.

c What proportion of the world's population is Chinese? Assume China's population is 1000 million and that world population is 5000 million.

4 a Choose one Asian and one African and one Latin American country from Table 5.4.
i For each, draw vertical bars to show average annual population percentage growth rates for urban and rural areas.
ii Colour all bars showing urban growth rates in one colour and rural growth rates in another. (If you choose Brazil, think how you can show its rural population rate of change. Perhaps you could draw your bar beneath a base line.)
iii Give your diagrams a heading.

b Write a note beneath the diagrams, commenting on the different population growth rates between urban and rural areas in your selected countries.
Suggest reasons for the differences – remember migration may be important too.

6 *Local population change*

People live where work is available. The population growth in towns often reflects available work and relative prosperity.

CASE STUDY *Merthyr Tydfil*

Look at Figure 6.1. See how the population has changed in Merthyr Tydfil, an industrial town in South Wales.

When iron ore and coal began to be mined in Merthyr Tydfil at the beginning of the nineteenth century, people moved there for paid work (see Fig. 6.2). The settlement grew from a village to a town by the twentieth century. Look at Figure 6.3 which shows such a change. Building a canal and a railway not only helped to move the iron and coal to markets but helped people move there too. This century the population has declined and labels on Figure 6.1 give some reasons for this.

CASE STUDY *Stevenage New Town*

Stevenage New Town in Hertfordshire, north of London, grew for a different reason. In 1947 the Government decided there should be several modern towns with good houses near places of work. Stevenage was one. This town's population grew from 6660 in 1951 to 74 513 in 1981.

Figure 6.1 The changing population and prosperity of Merthyr Tydfil 1750–1970.

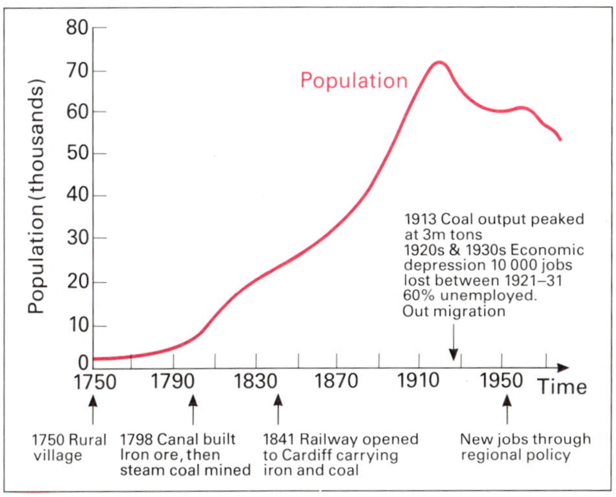

Figure 6.2 A coal mine in Merthyr Tydfil, 1913

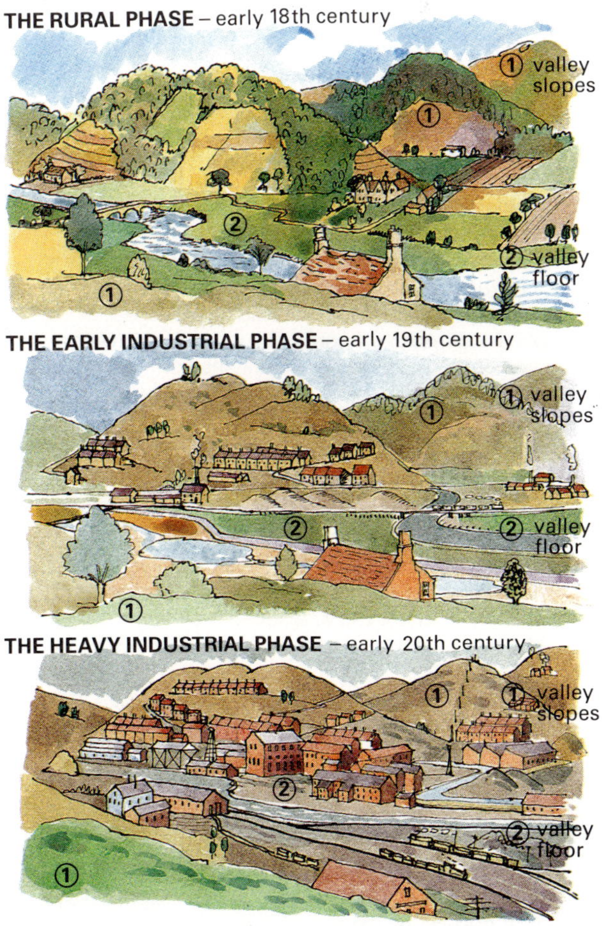

Figure 6.3 Population growth in a mining town.

Figure 6.4 A new pensioners' club in Stevenage

At first, most of Stevenage's population were young married couples and their children who moved from slums or bombed areas of London. Recently natural increase explains most of the population growth in the town. The town now has more retired people than it had twenty years ago for its population is ageing. The public services in the town, like numbers of primary schools and pensioners clubs (see Fig. 6.4), have had to change too.

ACTIVITIES

1 a Look at Fig. 6.5, the Ordnance Survey extract on a scale of 1:25 000 of part of the Rhondda valleys in South Wales. Find the location of this area in your atlas.

b On a piece of tracing paper placed over the Ordnance Survey extract shade in the areas of settlement in the Rhondda valleys. Name them.
  i In another colour, shade all quarries.
  ii Mark spoil heaps in another colour.
  iii Mark the location of mines (include disused).
  iv Make a key. Add the scale to your map. Show the direction of north. Give the map a title or heading explaining what it shows.

c Write a few sentences describing the location of the population of the area shown in the map extract. Suggest why people settled where they did.

d Draw a line graph to show population change in the Rhondda Borough from 1801 to 1986. Use the information in Table 6.1. You should put time on the horizontal or x axis but be careful after 1981! You must also think of a suitable vertical scale for the y axis on which to show population. Give the graph a title.
  Add labels to your graph commenting on trends in the population in the Rhondda Borough at different times.

e Look at Table 6.2. Compare the causes of death in 1900 with those in the Rhondda Borough in 1980. What factors may explain the differences?

f Why have many settlements in South Wales, like Merthyr Tydfil, and those in the Rhondda Valleys lost population since the 1920s?

Table 6.1 Population data for the Rhondda Borough

Year	Population
1801	542
1811	576
1821	647
1831	542
1841	748
1851	951
1861	3035
1871	23 950
1881	55 632
1891	88 351
1901	113 735
1911	152 781
1921	162 717
1931	141 346
1941	No data
1951	111 357
1961	100 314
1971	88 995
1981	81 725
1986	77 800

Source: Rhondda Borough Council

Table 6.2 Causes of death in the Rhondda Borough 1900 & 1980

1900		1980	
Cause	Numbers	Cause	Numbers
Measles	121	Infections & parasitic diseases	6
Scarlet fever	35	Cancer	230
Influenza	18	Endocrine, nutritional, metabolic and immunity disorders	4
Whooping cough	58	Disease of the blood	1
Diphtheria	125	Mental disorder	1
Enteric fever	24	Disease of nervous system	5
Dysentery	10	Disease of circulatory system	615
Enteritis	162	Disease of respiratory system	254
Erysipelas	1	Disease of digestive system	24
Puerperal fever	9	Disease of genito-urinary system	10
Other septic diseases	4	Disease of musculoskeletal system	4
Tuberculosis	141	Congenital abnormalities	2
Alcoholism	4	Perinatal conditions	14
Cancer	43	Injury and poisoning	28
Premature birth	66	Other conditions	16
Development diseases	230		
Old age	64		
Softening of the brain	8		
Heart disease	65		
Bronchitis	152		
Pneumonia	194		
Disease of the stomach	6		
Obstruction of intestines	16		
Cirrhosis of liver	10		
Bright's disease	42		
Female tumour	1		
Accident or negligence	101		
Suicide	2		
Other causes	11		

Source: Rhondda Borough Council

Figure 6.5

Different types of quarries

Disused pit or quarry

Refuse/slag heap

Chalk pit, clay pit or quarry

Coursework ideas

Find out from your school or public library the population changes in your home area such as your ward or district this century. Discover some key dates relating to changes in transport such as the coming of the railway or the opening of factories so that you can produce a graph rather like Figure 6.1 of Merthyr Tydfil.

7 Population and resources

Growth of world population has led people to wonder about the future. Look at Figure 7.1.

The Rev. **Thomas Malthus** took a gloomy view in 1798. He argued that the number of people would increase faster than food supplies. Starvation, war and disease would follow when the land could no longer support all the people. In other words the land had reached its **carrying capacity**.

Malthus believed that population growth might be checked if people married later and so had fewer children. Eventually, however, the lack of **resources** would limit the size of the population.

Read the article in Figure 7.2. Some aspects of recent famines in Ethiopia reflect Malthus' ideas. However, it is important to realise that drought, civil war and povery have reduced agricultural output.

Figure 7.1 One view of the future

In 1972 people from ten countries met in Rome. The group was known as **'The Club of Rome'**. They fed information into a computer in order to predict what may happen if world population and the use of resources continued to grow. The results are shown in Figure 7.3. Remember these are only predictions. They do suggest that if we continue to use the world's resources at the

Waiting at death's door

CATHARINE WATSON
reports from Adigudum

Ethiopia's drought was noticed on the day the last raindrop fell last July.

But Ethiopia still hangs by a thread. Aid workers say it would be fatal to relax. 'If we don't call it a catastrophe, it will become one,' said one worker in Tigray.

There are good reasons to worry. This year the food shortfall is greater, and the civil wars more intense, than during Ethiopia's last famine. And only one third of the 1.3 million tonnes of food that Ethiopia needs to survive until the next harvest in November has been promised by donors.

Tigray and Eritrea are the regions worst hit by the famine, too. Farmed for 3,000 years, they are beautiful but bleak: windswept, tree-less and rocky. The dust which gums the children's eyes shut is Ethiopia's topsoil, blowing into the waters of the Nile at the rate of over one billion tonnes a year.

Semerer Abreham is a 40-year-old peasant in Eritrea. In 1984, 80 per cent of his crop failed. This year the figure is 100 per cent. Adis Selassie, 37, who lives in Tigray, lost 40 per cent of his crop in the last drought; this year he lost 75 per cent.

Both are fatalistic and deeply attached to their land. Abreham believes the rains failed because people in his village mistrusted each other. 'Rains come when God wants,' he said. Selassie does not want to move to a greener, wetter and more fertile part of Ethiopia. 'Our culture does not allow us to freely go away,' he said, leaning on his donkey and waving at a barren stretch of land. 'This is the place of my grandmother.'

Thomas Grannel, of the World Food Programme, says simply: 'History has caught up with Ethiopia.' Eighty-eight per cent of the people, and 67 per cent of the 40 million animals, live in the eroded and deforested highlands. The land is exhausted.

Grannel's agency has spent $250 million and 12 years on planting trees and terracing. This, he says, has 'stabilised' 2.5 per cent of the seriously eroded land.

But for Ethiopia's 47 million people, seven million of whom now risk starvation, that pace is too slow. It cannot go any faster because Ethiopia is starved of funds for development. Britain, the US and most other Western countries give no development aid because of the Government's Marxist policies. Ethiopia receives only $9 per person per year in development aid: other poor African countries receive $20.

The crunch will come in February and March, when one million Tigreans now subsisting on their meagre harvest will suddenly need help.

The *Observer*
3.1.88

Figure 7.2

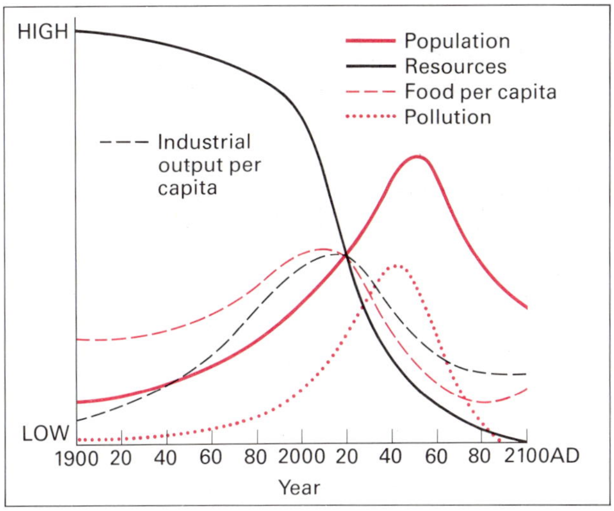

Figure 7.3 The limits to growth model of population development.

present rate the limits to growth on this planet will be reached in the next one hundred years as resources run out and pollution increases.

Many people believe that adequate food supplies already exist in the world. It is the distribution which is to blame with some groups receiving more than their fair share, while some receive less.

Another geographer, **Esther Boserup**, believes that a growing population forces farmers to adapt and change their methods. By doing this, higher yields are produced. In the Middle Ages in England farmers left a third of their land fallow in turn each year to keep it fertile. Now, using intensive methods and growing crops under glass, several harvests can be gained each year from an area of land (see Fig. 7.4).

ACTIVITIES

1 a Draw a graph to show how population might exceed food production over time according to Malthus. Put time on the horizontal x axis and growth rates for people and food supplies on the same vertical y axis. Assume the number of people increases at a geometric progression of 1, 2, 4, 8, 16, 32. The number doubles for each period of time such as every twenty years. Food supply increases over the same spans of time at an arithmetic progression of 1, 2, 3, 4, 5, 6. Plot a line to show how population grows over 100 years. On the same graph plot a line to show how food production grows over the same time period. Label each line. Label each axis. Give the diagram a title.

b By the graph, write two or three sentences describing the relationship between population and food supply according to Malthus.

2 a In 1798 Malthus predicted only a slow increase in food production. In fact, production has increased greatly. In groups or on your own, suggest reasons for this rather more rapid rate of increase than Malthus had expected.

b Collect pictures and articles from papers and magazines to make a display showing modern methods of food production.

3 a Read Figure 7.2. Which parts of Ethiopia are short of food and suffering from famine?

b Make a list of the reasons why Ethiopia is short of food. Is rapid population growth the sole cause?

c Discuss and then write down what you would do to relieve hunger in Ethiopia in the short term if you were in charge of a relief programme.

d What long-term development schemes could you suggest which would benefit the people of Ethiopia in the future?

4 a Look at Figure 7.3 showing the results of 'The Club of Rome's' predictions. Discuss why the pollution curve follows the population curve.

b Make a list of as many types of pollution that people cause as you can.

c Write down examples of pollution of the air, water and land found between your home and school or in or near your school grounds.

Figure 7.4 Fertile land by the River Nile allows intensive farming

8 The Demographic Transition Theory

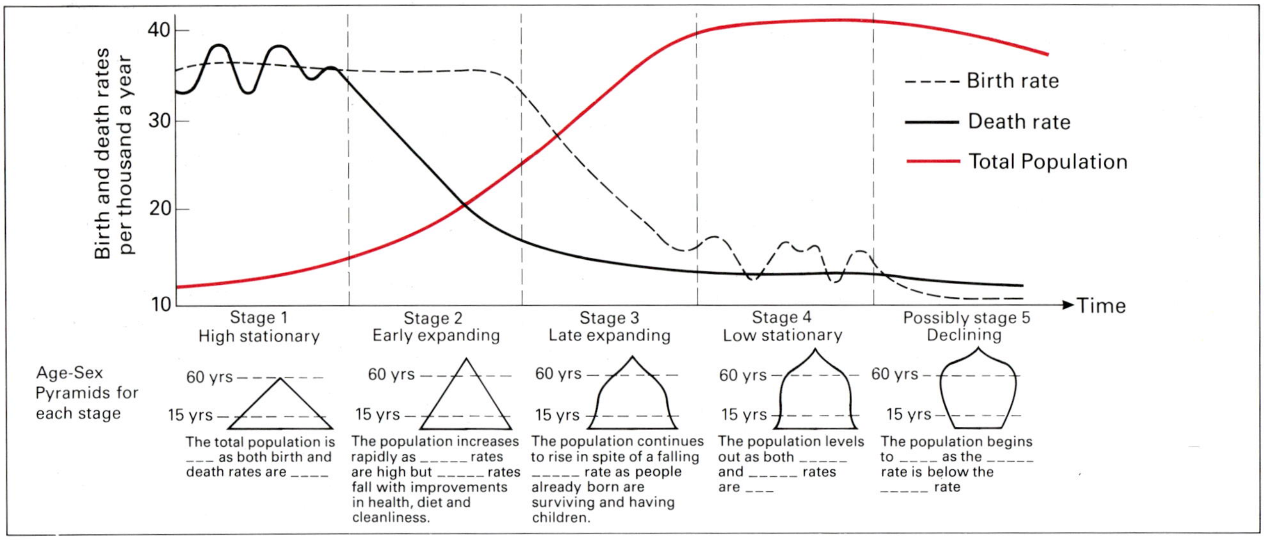

Figure 8.1 The Demographic Transition Theory.

A more hopeful prediction for the fate of the world's population is the **Demographic Transition Theory**. It is based on evidence of falling death rates and later falling birth rates in Western Europe since the early nineteenth century. Look at Figure 8.1. It suggests that the population of a country or area goes through four or even five stages. Eventually population growth stabilises or decreases.

At first, although many are born, the population remains low as there is a high death-rate. Secondly, when the death rate falls through better food, health and hygiene, the population increases rapidly. In time, realising children are surviving, people have fewer babies. Contraception helps this. Although the birth rate falls, the population total continues to increase as many people are in the reproductive age-group. The fourth stage of the theory is reached when the total population stabilises. A possible fifth stage is when the total population declines with birth rates below death rates.

Although this is an optimistic theory it may not be true and may not apply to all countries such as in the developing world. Time will tell!

ACTIVITIES

1 a Make a copy of Figure 8.1 showing the Demographic Transition Theory. Complete the description under each stage by filling in the blanks.

b Shade in the natural increase of population on the diagram – (the gap between the birth rate and death rate.)

2 Look at the population pyramids for England and Wales in 1901 and 1981 in Figure 2.1.

a In which stage would you put the pyramid for 1901?

b In which stage would you put the pyramid for 1981?

c Is it easy to fit a pyramid shape for an actual country to a stage in the theory? What other information might you need?

3 Look at Figure 2.3.

a In which stage of the theory would you place the population pyramid for Nigeria?

b Explain your reasons.

c In which stage of the theory would you place the population pyramid for West Germany?

d What do you predict may happen to the total population of West Germany in the next twenty years?

9 Policies of population control

'One child only' slogan spreads across China

By NIGEL WADE in Peking

THE slogan, "It is best to have only one child and two at most," is spreading across China as more and more provinces adopt birth control incentives and economic sanctions against couples having more than the approved number of children.

A series of strict birth control measures has been announced in several parts of China.

Coupons awarded

It is now official policy to reward couples who have only one child and undertake not to have more. Some provinces give these couples a "planned parenthood honour" coupon, which ensures priority for their child in education and medical care.

Couples having only one child will receive the same housing floorspace as couples having two, and an only child will receive an adult's grain ration.

To placate couples in conservative peasant areas where male children are traditionally preferred the new birth control measures provide preferential pension terms for peasants having only daughters. This is to stop them going on having children until they get a son to support them in their old age.

Couples in some provinces who produce a second child after being rewarded for undertaking to have only one will have their rewards revoked and will also be required to pay a surcharge for their children's health expenses.

Too many children

The surcharge will rise to seven per cent of the parents' combined monthly income if they have as many as five children.

Couples having three or more will be denied extra living space and extra food ration tickets.

A Peking birth control official said recently that the old belief that every family should have a son was still common, and that about 15 per cent. of all rural households had too many children.

China wants to cut its population growth rate to less than one per cent. a year by 1980.

The average annual population growth rate in recent years has been about two per cent., which is higher than the rate of growth in grain production.

Figure 9.2
The *Daily Telegraph*, **June 5 1979**

Lu Bo is a twenty-nine year old cashier in a hotel in Jinxian county in Liaoning Province in China. Her child has just had her first birthday. Lu said that last year she only worked for seven months. The rest she took off to have the baby. As a result her income was reduced. As her husband's wages are low she does not want another child.

In the past, many Chinese like Lu Bo had more children in the hope of having a boy. On marrying she would have gone to live with her husband's family.

Lu Bo and others like her now want to work and have their own homes. They want to buy furniture and improve their homes. The Chinese Government is encouraging directly people like Lu Bo to have small families.

Governments may introduce policies to control population growth in their countries. China and India are both trying to limit their populations: they have **anti-natalist policies**.

Lu Bo and other young Chinese like her have been encouraged since 1979 by the Government to have only one child.

The Chinese Government was alarmed that it might not be able to feed and support its population. Look back to Table 5.2. You learnt in the section on 'Population Growth and Change' that China's population went from 542 million in 1949 to nearly 1000 million in 1981. This growth was due to a high birth-rate and a falling death-rate.

Figure 9.1 Advertising a one child per family policy in China

In 1979 China began an anti-natalist policy. A man cannot now marry until he is twenty-two and a woman cannot marry until she is twenty. The couple are urged to have only one child (see Fig. 9.1). Remember Mamtaz whom you read about in Chapter 3. She was married at thirteen and had six children by her early twenties! Read Figure 9.2 to find out the rewards and penalties linked to China's policy.

By 1984 the unpopular policy of one child per couple was relaxed for some people. Those allowed to apply for permission to have a second child include couples who were both only children, rural couples where one or the other has a parent who was an only child and only sons who have fathered a daughter.

The official reason for the change in policy is that many females died in a famine from 1959–61. Therefore there are fewer women to have children than had been expected.

Look at Figure 9.3. It shows computer predictions of China's future population structure if the birth rate falls. Notice the population pyramids A and C for the year 2000. If each female has one child many old people will need to be looked after by fewer young people.

Figure 9.3 Projected population pyramids for China if population policies are continued for 100 years.

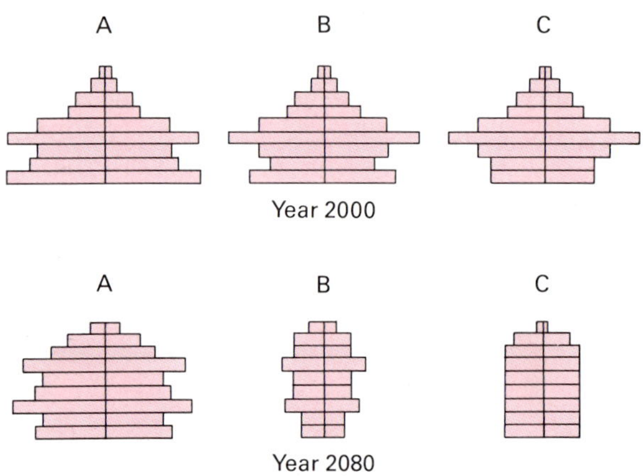

Projection A assumes that each female has on average two children

Projection B assumes that each female has on average 1.5 children

Projection C assumes that each female has 1 or no more than 1.8 children

India has had family planning services since 1930. Between 1972 and 1977 sterilizations (especially of males since the operation is simpler than for females) were carried out. Sterilizations, making people infertile, were at first on volunteers. By 1975 many were forced to be sterilized, it is claimed, against their will. The outcry against these acts helped lead to a change of Government in 1977. Perhaps more importantly, however, it has been a severe set back to the cause of population control.

ACTIVITIES

1 Form discussion groups of three or four pupils each representing the Government of a developing country. Each group should appoint one person to present their views to the class at the end. You are to discuss the following proposals and decide which *five* in rank order should be introduced to improve the standard of living of the population. Most are very poor peasant farmers with large families. You cannot afford to introduce more than five schemes at once. You must also consider the likely long-term effects of your actions.
   - a Send abroad fifty of your best students to be trained as doctors, engineers, teachers and nurses.
   - b Provide free education for all children up to the age of fourteen.
   - c Purchase and run ten mobile health caravans to reach the more remote parts of the country.
   - d Immunise all children against polio, malaria, whooping cough, measles and tetanus.
   - e Introduce and run mobile family planning services to reach women in rural areas.
   - f Provide a small pension for all elderly people over the age of sixty-five years.
   - g Lay a clean, piped water supply throughout the capital city.

2 Watch television advertisements involving families. Record the number of children shown in each family. What do you find advertisers regard as the typical family size in the United Kingdom?

3 a Read Figure 9.2. Make a list of the benefits the Chinese were offered after 1979 if they agreed to have only one child.
   - b Make a list of what penalties would be imposed if they had more than one child.

4 Imagine you are the third child in a large family of seven children in a developing country. Make two lists:
   - i giving the advantages of being part of a large family;
   - ii the disadvantages of being part of a large family.

10 Policies of population growth

Chirac : « La famille est prioritaire »

Le premier ministre veut poursuivre en ce sens une politique «résolue et ambitieuse» pour endiguer le déclin démographique.

Dans son projet de gouvernement, Jacques Chirac a aussi des priorités et, pour lui, il l'a dit hier, la priorité des priorités c'est une politique « résolue et ambitieuse en faveur de la famille ». « Toute l'expérience de l'histoire de nos civilisations, a-t-il déclaré, montre que chaque fois que la cellule familiale s'est dégénérée, cela s'est traduit par un déclin de la civilisation. Nous sommes en période de déclin démographique. C'est dangereux et c'est mortel. Nous avons une responsabilité à l'égard de nos petits-enfants. On ne peut pas, après avoir hérité une France belle et forte, qu'elle l'a été dans les années soixante, nous désintéresser de la France que nous allons léguer à nos enfants et à nos petits-enfants. Une France ou une Europe en voie de décomposition serait alors colonisée par d'autres... »

Le Figaro, 6.3.88

Figure 10.1 ▼ Figure 10.2 ▲

France cheers le bébé boom

For centuries the French have worried about their birthrate. Now things are looking up at last, reports JOHN IZBICKI

For the third year in succession, the French population is on the increase.

By the year 2020, France will become the most populated country in the EEC, with 58.6 million, compared with 55 million in 1985. The UK, believe it or not, follows closely, rising from 56.5 million in 1985 to 58.5 million in 2020. Germany, however, over the same period, is set to plummet from 61 million to 51 million.

Now why, you might well ask, should this mini-explosion in France's birthrate alongside West Germany's clear dip, bring joy to the French? According to M. Michel Lévy, the French "believe subconsciously that a small population makes a country weak in every sense".

He goes further: "Many Frenchmen and women are convinced that France suffered disastrously in battles with and under the occupation of the Germans in both the first and second world wars because the German population was bigger than the French and that the failure to produce more children led to the nation's punishment."

This obsession with the number of children each woman should bear has been a French trait for many centuries. When the Black Death stalked Europe, Britain's population was about three million; France had some 20 million and was able to face the killer disease more easily than its neighbours.

The French are by no means alone in holding the view that there is strength in numbers and that a country's defence as well as its economy will prosper once its population has grown. This week, Lee Kwan Yew, Singapore's prime minister, appealed to the city-state's womenfolk to produce an additional 40,000 babies within 10 years to stop the population from growing "dangerously low".

Can a population not also grow "dangerously high"? China might have views to offer on that question. So might Miss Yu Xiao Zhan, a young Chinese woman who turned up in a Lille court on Wednesday charged with working without a permit. She claimed she had come to France to start a *famille nombreuse* (large family) — an ambition not permissible in China.

Mme Michèle Barzach, the Minister of Health and Population (the very fact that there is a Minister of Population says something . . .) feels that France could and should do better. "The increase is still too small to allow for the renewal of the population," she says.

The birthrate among Frenchwomen of child-bearing age has increased from 1.82 children per woman to 1.84 over the past three years. For the population to remain stable, that birthrate should rise to at least 2.1 children apiece.

How do these figures compare with the rest of Europe? In Holland it is 1.51, in Norway 1.66, in Sweden 1.74, in Italy 1.4, in Portugal 1.8, and in Spain it has shown another steep slide from 2.35 in 1979 to 1.65 in 1984. West Germany has already reached what is considered to be its lowest individual birthrate figure with 1.28 in 1985, while the figure in East Germany, whose ideas on population resemble those of France and Singapore and whose policies encourage child-bearing, has risen from 1.54 in 1975 to 1.94 in 1980.

Well ahead of all its EEC partners, with 2.54 (in 1984), is Ireland.

Telegraph 22.8.87

Figure 10.3 *Sunday Times* 24.2.85

Romanians chafe at baby drive

by Peter Godwin
Bucharest

THE PEOPLE of Romania were last week given a pat on the head by President Nicolae Ceausescu for their progress towards yet another target: the production of more babies. Worried by Romania's flagging population, he chose the occasion of international women's day last year to order his citizens to go forth and multiply. Every couple should have at least four.

Last week he announced that the population growth rate was up to 5.2 per 1,000 last year, compared with 3.9 in 1983, the lowest since the war. Population has increased to 22,687,374.

However, the achievement was not altogether voluntary.

Artificial contraceptives have been banned and abortion, once the most common form of birth-control in Romania, is denied to most women.

Initially the president was rewarded with a rise in the birth rate from 6.1 to 18.1 per 1000, but it soon slid down again as doctors ignored the regulations.

By 1983 the authorities estimated that, of 742,882 registered pregnancies, 321,598 resulted in live births and the other 421,384 were aborted, only 9% of them for legal reasons. Including unrecorded pregnancies and backstreet abortions, the ratio of live births to abortions was estimated at about 1:4.

The president warned doctors that abortion legislation must be followed to the letter. Doctors who fail to justify abortions they perform are imprisoned for up to three years and struck off the register. Patients face heavy fines and up to two years in jail.

Under the population drive, young women are obliged to undergo regular pregnancy tests and, once registered as pregnant, are watched carefully to ensure they do not get rid of the baby. Any termination of pregnancy is closely investigated.

Contraceptives have been banned and can be obtained only on the black market.

Those not married by 25 pay an extra 8% to 10% in penalty tax. They cannot apply for housing and in practice their careers suffer through lack in promotion. They are not considered for trips abroad.

Television campaigns have been screened and government doctors preach the virtues of big families in factories, offices and schools. The legal marrying age for girls was dropped from 18 to 15 and attempts made to remove the stigma of unmarried motherhood. Special classes for pregnant schoolgirls have been organised to permit them to continue their schooling after the birth. Fertility clinics have been set up around the country to investigate failure to conceive.

As incentives, women are given generous maternity leave on full pay, a reduction in working hours with no salary loss after the birth, and special paid leave to look after sick children. They also get a lump sum bonus as a reward. Non-working mothers also get a lump-sum for each baby, plus a monthly payment for each child.

This extensive package of measures, however, has done little to tackle the underlying causes of Romania's population decline. For many Romanians, huddled in freezing, overcrowded apartments, queuing for food and struggling to make ends meet, more children is the last thing they need. Overhasty industrialisation and the rush to towns has resulted in one of the lowest standards of living, in real terms, in eastern Europe.

As with most things, the Romanian government has grand five year plans for population growth: by the end of this year the population target is 23.4 m, rising through 25 m in 1990 to 30 m by the year 2000.

Six-year old Peter in Bavaria, West Germany, was looking forward to his first day at school. Football was his favourite game. However, he came home crying from school at the end of the day. There were not enough in his class to form a team of eleven.

Some countries like West Germany, France and Romania in the developed world and Singapore and Malaysia in the less developed world are trying to encourage the growth of their populations or sections of their populations. They have **pro-natalist policies**.

One reason Peter had so few class mates is because few children are being born in West Germany. Since 1974 there have been years when the birth rate is lower than the death rate.

Chancellor Kohl stated in 1983 that the Republic of West Germany 'must again foster a positive attitude towards children. Families will continue to receive assistance in the form of child benefits and tax relief.' To encourage larger families in 1987 the state paid DM 50 per month for a first child, DM 100 for the second, DM 220 for the third and DM 240 for the fourth and every child after that until the age of eighteen years. Benefits and tax relief continue to the age of twenty-seven years if that person is in training. Rent allowances, reduced fares on public transport and student loans are financial supports for large families.

Look at Figures 10.1 and 10.2. Read them carefully to find out why France believes it is necessary to have a growing population.

Romania, as a European communist state, had a pro-natalist policy from 1965. Read Figure 10.3. It describes why and how Romania encouraged more births under Ceausescu.

Singapore in the developing world tried in 1966 to limit the size of families to two children. Since 1983 the state has wanted graduates to marry and have children. The Government thinks this might improve the intelligence of the population! A slogan encourages the intelligent with the words: 'At least two. Better three. Four if you can afford it.' It is believed a larger population would stimulate economic growth (see Fig. 10.4).

The Prime Minister of Malaysia has gone further by encouraging Malaysian families since 1982 to 'Go for five!' children. Malaysia's population is less than 16 million people. The authorities think the country could support seventy million people! They say 'seventy million people working very hard and producing a lot of goods could easily live in Malaysia – and even produce sufficient food.'

More people would make more goods, perhaps for export. More people would need more goods and services and so stimulate industries. More jobs would be created. In this way the economy might spiral upwards.

To encourage larger Malaysian families, maternity benefits and tax concessions are granted. It has been suggested that the bumiputera (the local Malays) are encouraged to have larger families than the immigrant Chinese and Indians. In this way most of the population would be Malay.

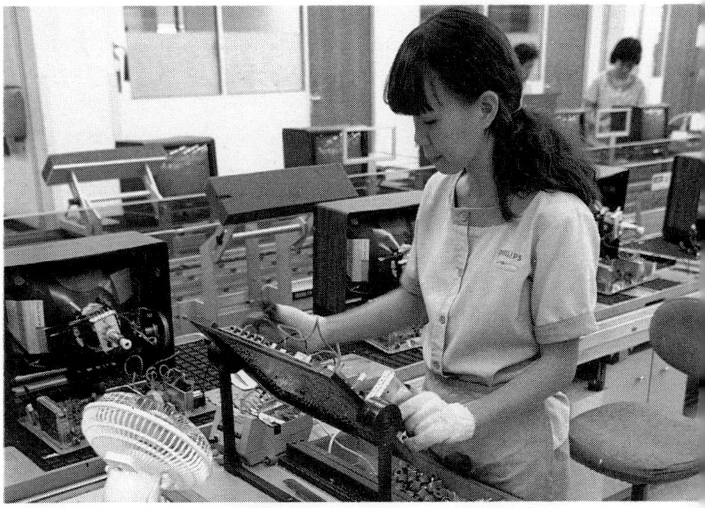

Figure 10.4 A young worker in Singapore

ACTIVITIES

1 Imagine you are an only child aged fourteen of parents in their late forties in West Germany. Make two lists:
   a giving the advantages of being in a small family;
   b giving the disadvantages of being in a small family.

2 Using Figures 10.2 and 10.5, explain why the French feel they need a big population.

3 a Read Figure 10.3. Write down why Romanians were urged to have at least four children.
   b How did Romania try to increase the number of births in recent years?

4 Make a poster urging people to have more babies in West Germany or France or Singapore or Malaysia. It should suggest why population growth is needed in your chosen country.

Figure 10.5 France wants more babies

11 Controlling immigration

Figure 11.1 Party-going in Brixton

Figure 11.2 USA citizens are of many ethnic groups

Look at Figure 11.1. A street party was held in Brixton in South London in June 1988. It was held to celebrate the arrival, forty years ago, of West Indian workers to Britain. At that time in the late 1940s there was a shortage of unskilled workers. Organisations like London Transport needed workers. Men were recruited in the Caribbean where there was high unemployment to work in Britain. Many brought their families.

In the last forty years many other immigrant groups such as European and Kampuchean refugees settled in Britain. Asians from East Africa and India, Bangladesh and Pakistan have come to Britain. Many could settle here because they were Commonwealth citizens. They held a British passport. Some had been forced to leave some African states. In 1972 about 25 000 British Asians came to Britain, expelled from Uganda. Look at Table 2.4. You will see that now in Britain large percentages of children aged under fifteen years are of immigrant origin.

Governments place **controls on migration** sometimes within states or across their borders. If you have been abroad, you will know that on leaving or entering a country passport checks are made. Sometimes a visa or work permit is needed before entry is possible. Countries like the USA and the USSR have strict controls on who enters or leaves.

In 1962 the Commonwealth Immigrants Act was passed in the United Kingdom. That Act and those passed afterwards in 1968, 1971 and 1982 limited the numbers and types of immigrants into Britain. People allowed in had jobs to come to or particular skills or rights of citizenship. A **citizen** is a native or member of a state with certain rights such as to vote in elections. Now, if children are born abroad even though their parents are British they may not be able to be British citizens.

113 000 British citizens and 130 000 **aliens** or non-British people entered the United Kingdom in the year ending June 1986. In the same year 106 000 British citizens and 70 000 non-British people left the country. There was therefore a **net gain** of 67 000 people through migration. A net gain means there were more entering than leaving the country.

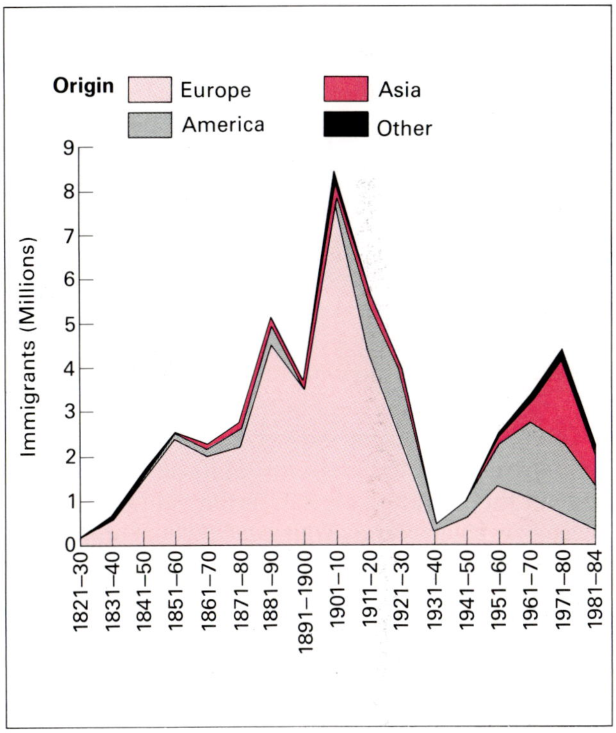

Figure 11.3 The origin of immigrants to the USA 1821–1984.

CASE STUDY *Immigration in USA*

President Kennedy in the 1960s, who was himself the grandson of an Irish immigrant, said that the United States of America was 'a society of immigrants' (see Fig. 11.2.).

In the nineteenth century millions of immigrants entered the USA. The population was seventy-six million in 1900. It rose to 151 million in 1950 and was about 240 million in 1986. Look at Figure 11.3 and see the numbers and origin of immigrants to the USA. Probably over fifty-one million people entered the USA between 1820 and 1984. Between 1925 and 1965 a quota system existed. It meant that only limited numbers of people from certain countries could enter. The numbers were in proportion to the nationalities in the USA in 1920. You will see in Figure 11.3, eighty-seven per cent of all immigrants to the USA at that time were from the United Kingdom, Ireland, Germany and Scandinavia. Refugees were allowed in as a special group after World War II.

In 1965 the quota system was abolished. The Act replacing it permits 270 000 people into the USA a year. Priority is given to single adults who are children of American citizens. As in Britain, people with special skills like scientists, doctors and nurses are also given priority.

ACTIVITIES

1. If you or your parents have a passport, look at what it states about you and what it requests.
2. Look at the photographs 11.1 and 11.2. Why are some immigrants more obvious than others?
3. Discuss in your class the following issues:
   a. do you think children of immigrants should have their school lessons in the language of the country they have moved to?
   b. if over fifty per cent of children in a school are of one immigrant group, do you think they should have their lessons in their native language or in the language of the country they have moved to? Explain clearly the reasons for your views.
4. Look at the advertisement in Figure 11.4.
   a. Why do you think it necessary for many job advertisements to state they are willing to consider applications from people regardless of creed or ethnic origin?
   b. What is racism? How can the police help fight racism?
5. Discuss in class or hold a debate on whether you think any political group which is against a multi-racial or **plural society** should be banned. Give your reasons.

Figure 11.4

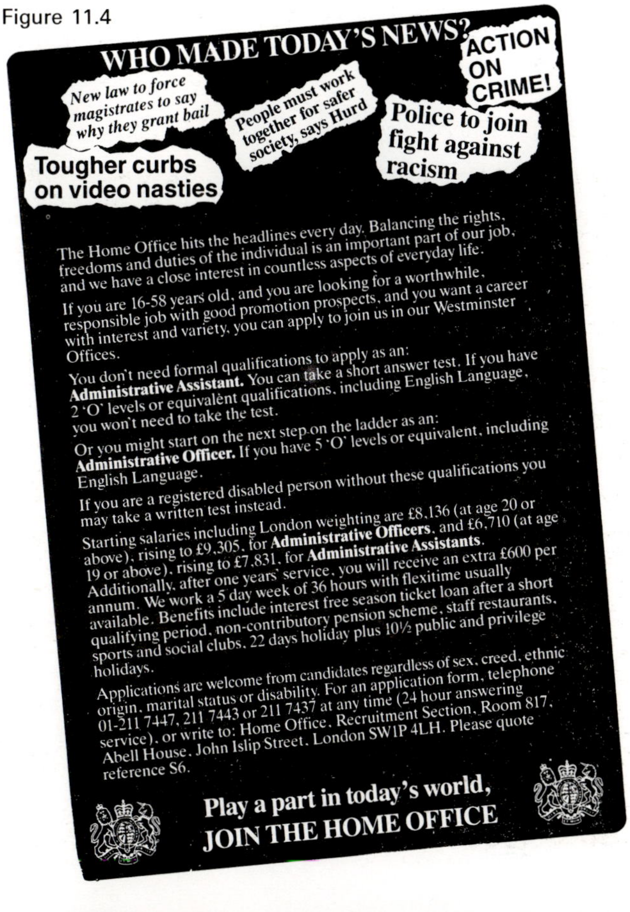

12 Factors influencing population distribution

Look at Figure 12.1, the Map extract. It shows part of the Hardanger Fjord in Western Norway. Locate the fjord in your atlas. Notice that settlement is unevenly spaced across the map.

People have always tried to live where **resources** provide them with fresh water, food, shelter and work. (See 'Settlement site' in the *Settlement* book).

Figure 12.1 Part of the Hardanger Fjord, 1:50,000

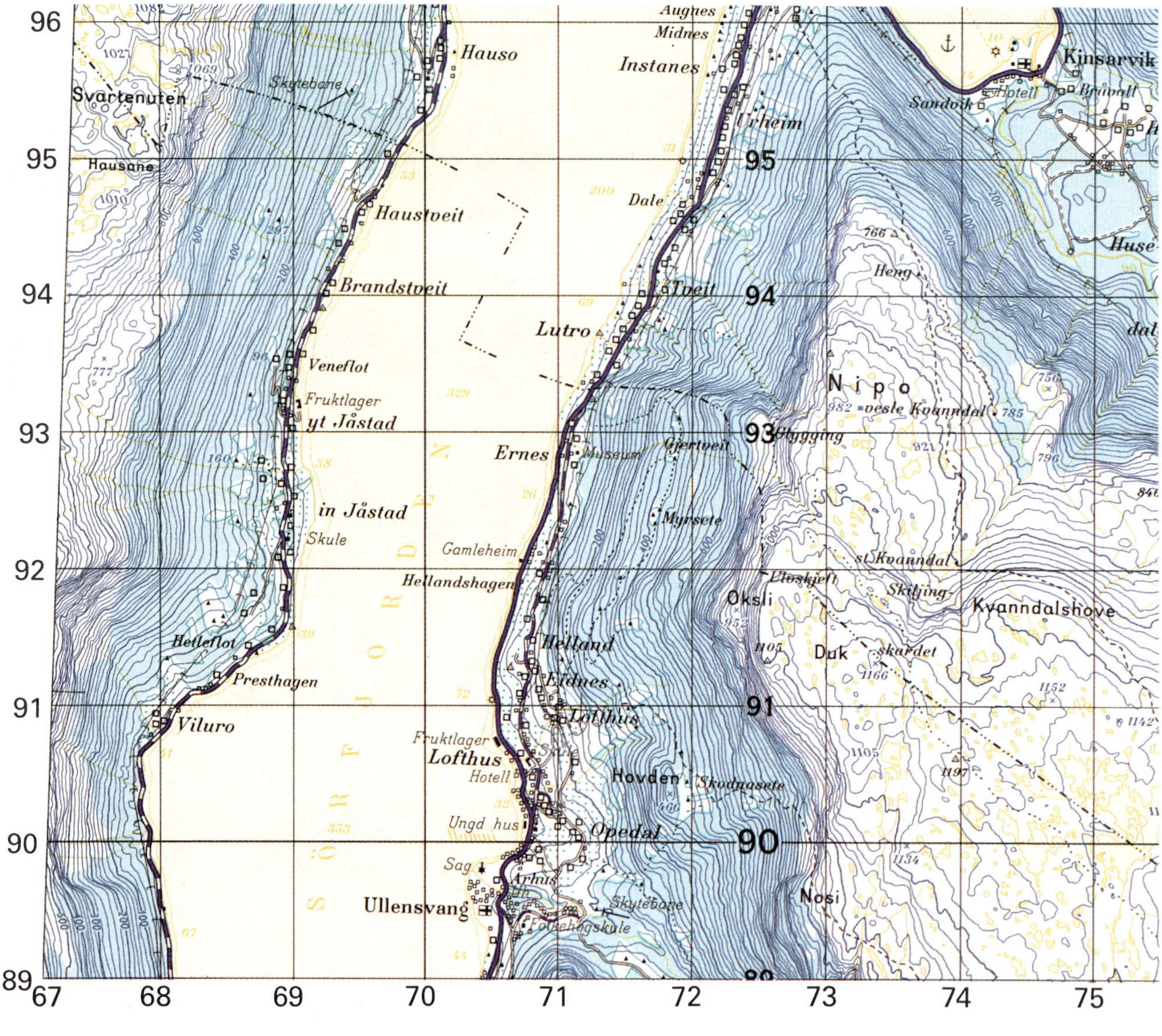

Resources and other geographical advantages are unevenly spread across the earth. As a result some areas are more thickly populated than others. Eighty per cent of the world's population live on less than twenty per cent of the land surface.

The Norwegian map extract shows that settlements tend to be at a low altitude, by the edge of the fjord and on flat, fertile, alluvial fans such as at Ullensvang. Transport by boat along the fjord and by the coast are important links between settlements. A few cabins and huts are on slopes up to about 400 or 500 m above sea level, but above that, there is little settlement (see Fig. 12.2). Favourable settlement sites for the 4.1 million Norwegians are in short supply. Over seventy per cent of the country is glaciers, lakes or barren areas, fifty per cent is north of the Arctic Circle. Twenty five per cent is over 1000 m above sea level.

Population density is a useful expression for describing and comparing population distribution. Imagine that the squares in Figure 12.3 represent a deserted island to which the settlers, seen arriving by boat, spread evenly over the land. It is easy to see that on average there would be two people on every square kilometre of territory. Population density can be calculated as:

$$\textbf{Population density} = \frac{\textbf{Population}}{\textbf{Area}}$$

Figure 12.3 Population density.

Figure 12.2 Part of the Hardanger Fjord

ACTIVITIES

1 a Draw a cross-section from the Norwegian map extract from 671897 to 738897. You need only mark the contours at every 100 m. Use a vertical scale on your cross-section frame of 1 cm to 200 m and a horizontal scale of 2 cm to 1 km or 1000 m.

b Mark and name the location of the fjord, the area of settlement, the road, the forested slopes, the plateau. Remember to make the scales, label each axis and put a heading on your section.

2 a Describe and suggest reasons for the location of Kinsarvik in the Kinso Valley on the Norwegian map. Try to explain why more houses are on the north-east side of the valley. How may aspect affect settlement?

b Describe and explain the pattern of communications. Why are ferry routes important (742958, dotted line)?

13 Global distribution of population

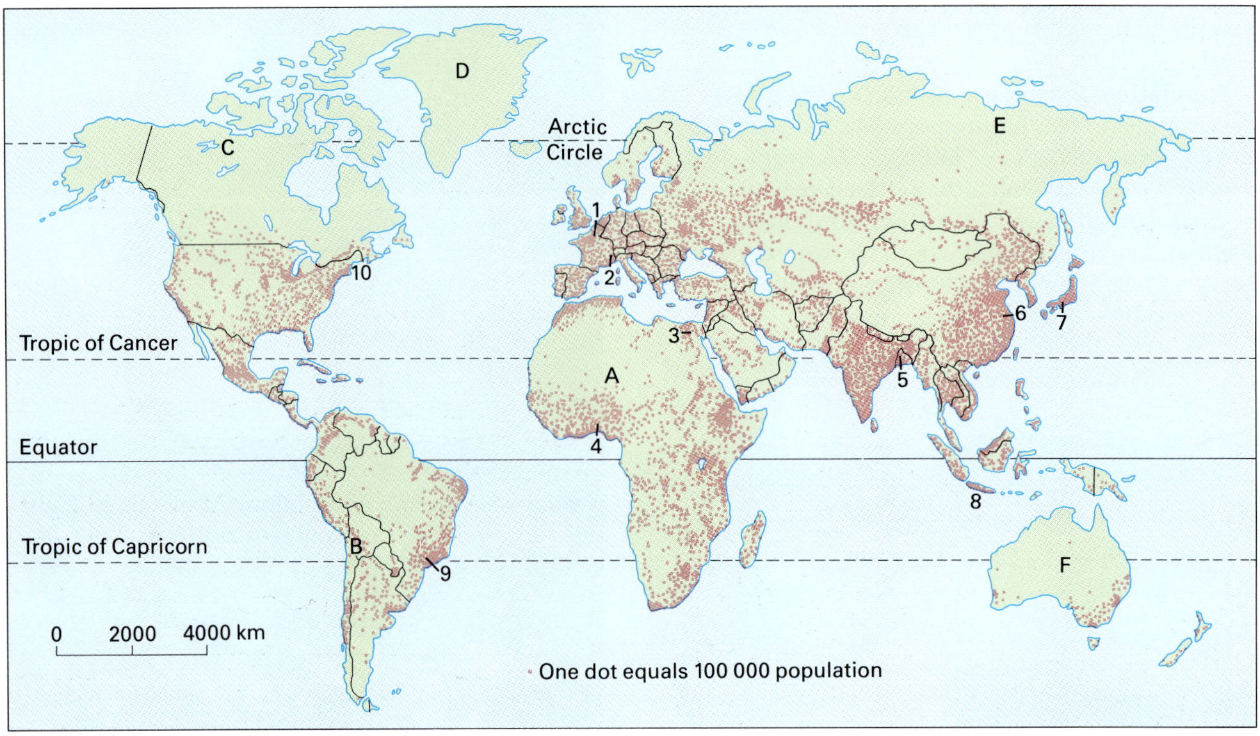

Figure 13.1 World population distribution.

Look at the **dot map** on Figure 13.1. It shows, using dots, where most people live in the world. One dot represents 100 000 people. The map can only give a very general impression of where people live.

It is clear that much of the land is virtually uninhabited. In fact about sixty per cent of the land has no people on it. Most of these areas are hostile to settlement. The hot desert areas (see Fig. 13.2) like the Sahara Desert have few people. Cold desert areas too like north of the Arctic Circle in Canada (see Fig. 13.3) have few people living there. High, steep slopes, such as on the Andes and Himalayas have few people. Small clusters of people may be found where resources like oil or minerals are extracted, but they do not show up on a map like this.

Figure 13.2
Low density settlement in the Sahara

About seventy per cent of the world's population live in fertile lowlands in:

1 Western Europe, like the River Rhine delta area in the Netherlands (see Fig. 14.3);
2 Asia, like the River Ganges and Brahmaputra deltas in India and Bangladesh and in valleys in eastern China;
3 North eastern North America near New York and Boston.

Smaller concentrations of people live:

a near the coast in parts of South America (see Fig. 13.4) and
b Australia;
c in the Nile valley in Africa (see Fig. 7.4); by water and other resources in Central Africa.

You will notice that most people – in fact over ninety per cent – live in the northern hemisphere where most of the land is found.

Figure 13.4 High density Settlement in Rio de Janeiro

Figure 13.3 Low density Settlement in The Canadian Arctic

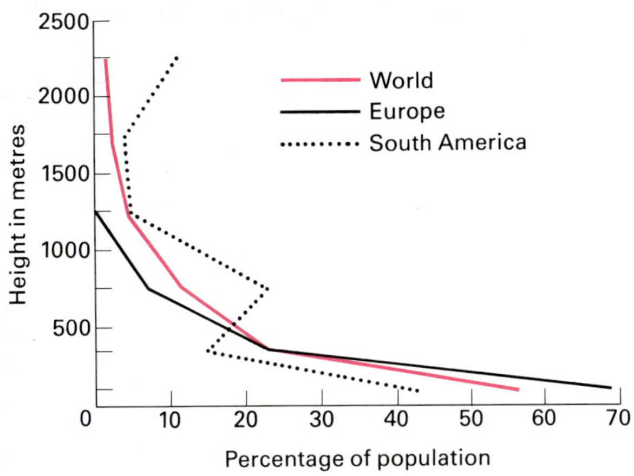

Figure 13.5 The vertical distribution of population.

Look at Figure 13.5. Most of the world's population live at altitudes below 500 m. A height of about 5000 m is generally the limit of comfortable human occupation. Above that height, low oxygen levels and low temperatures make life difficult.

ACTIVITIES

1 a On a world outline map mark the main areas of population from Figure 13.1. Insert the equator, the tropics, the Arctic and Antarctic circles and the 0° line of longitude.
  b Name the areas of dense population labelled 1–10 using your atlas. Mark these on your map.
  c Name the areas of sparse population labelled A–F using your atlas. Mark these on your map.
  d With the help of this section and an atlas try to explain why the following areas have many people:
    i the coastal areas of the Netherlands and South East England;
    ii the Nile delta and valley in Egypt;
    iii the Ganges and Brahmaputra deltas in India and Bangladesh;
    iv the island of Java in Indonesia.
  e With the help of this section and an atlas try to explain why the following areas have few people:
    i a large area of Africa on the Tropic of Cancer;
    ii the northern coastal areas of the USSR;
    iii the Andes in South America.

2 What are the disadvantages of dot maps in showing population distribution or location?

14 Population distribution in Europe

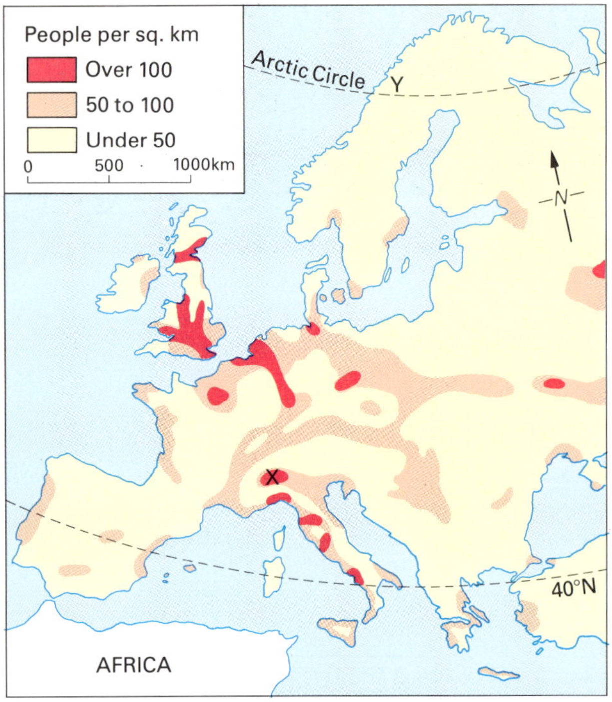

Figure 14.1 Where people live in Europe.

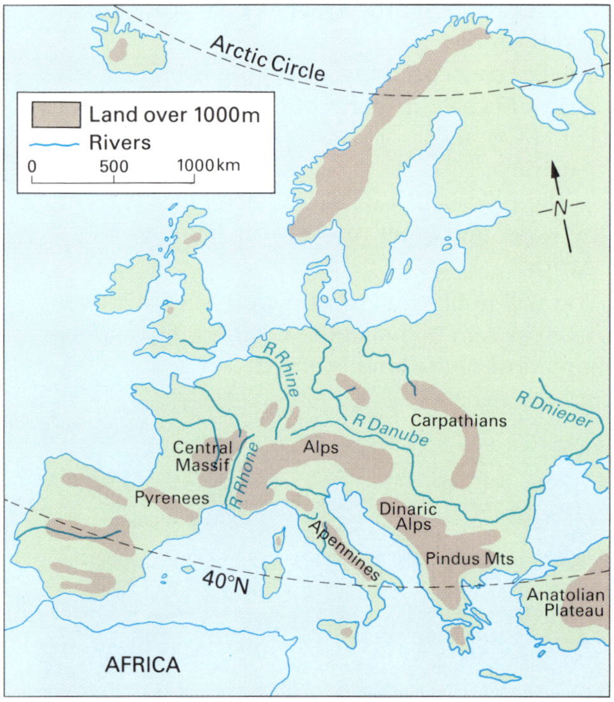

Figure 14.2 Physical geography of Europe.

Figure 14.1 shows where people live in Europe. As you can see, there are areas where there are over 100 people on every square kilometre of land. There are larger areas with fewer people to each square kilometre.

Compare the map of where people live in Figure 14.1 with the physical map of Europe Figure 14.2. The areas of high population density of over fifty people per kilometre square occur in strips mostly running west to east through comparatively low land in central Europe (see Fig. 14.3). Some river valleys, like the Rhine, where resources of water, fertile silt, minerals and good transport occur, have also attracted settlement. Coastal areas of the English Channel and the Mediterranean where trade has occurred have pockets of high population density.

The areas of lowest densities are on highland above 1000 m and in high altitudes where winters are long and cold (see Fig 14.4).

Figure 14.3 Concentration of settlement in the Randstadt near the mouth of the Rhine

Look at Table 14.1. You will see that the area and population size of each country in Europe vary very much.

ACTIVITIES

1 a Trace Figure 14.2 of the physical map of Europe. Use an atlas to name all rivers and mountain areas shown. Add a title. Include a key if necessary.

b On a piece of tracing paper copy the outline of Europe from Figure 14.1 and shade the areas where over fifty people per kilometre square live. Add a title. Make a key.

c Fasten the traced map of where people live in Europe exactly *over* the map of the physical geography of Europe. (Only fasten one side of the traced map so that you can use the two together, or the physical one alone.)

d With the help of your maps drawn in exercises **a**, **b** and **c**, an atlas and other reference books, try to explain:

i why many people live in area X on Figure 14.1;

ii why few people live in area Y on Figure 14.1.

2 Look at Figure 13.5 in the previous chapter.

a What percentage of Europe's population live above 1000 m?

b What percentage of Europeans prefer to live in areas under 1000 m? Suggest reasons for this.

3 Look at Table 14.1 showing the area and population of European countries.

a Copy and complete Table 14.1 by working out population densities. Some have been done for you. Look back to the text on page 35 to find out how to calculate population density.

b On an outline map of European countries, (one is in the *Teachers' Book*), show by four types of shading the average population density for each country.

i Use a light shade for countries with average densities of under 100 people per kilometre square.

ii Use a slightly heavier shade for countries with average densities of 100 to 199 people per kilometre square.

iii Use heavier shading for countries with average densities of 200 to 350 people per kilometre square.

iv Use the heaviest or darkest colour for countries with average densities of over 350 people per kilometre square.

Remember to give your map a title and a key.

c Choose one country with a low density and one with a high density. Try to suggest reasons for the difference in density. Use your atlas to help you.

d Why does your map of population densities in each European country give a misleading picture of where people really live?

Figure 14.4 The empty, high plateau of Norway

Table 14.1 Area and population of European countries (1984)

Country	Area in 000s of km^2	Population in millions	Population density per km^2
Albania	27	2.9	107
Austria	83	7.6	92
Belgium	30	9.9	330
Bulgaria	111	9.0	81
Czechoslovakia	125	15.4	123
Denmark	42	5.1	
Finland	305	4.9	
France	546	54.9	
German Democratic Republic	106	16.6	
German Federal Republic	244	61.1	
Greece	131	9.9	
Hungary	92	10.0	
Iceland	100	2.4	
Ireland (Irish Republic)	69	3.5	
Italy	294	57.0	
Luxembourg	2.6	0.3	
Malta	0.3	0.4	
Netherlands	34	14.4	424
Norway	308	4.1	13
Poland	305	36.9	121
Portugal	92	10.1	
Romania	230	22.9	
Spain	499	36.7	
Sweden	412	8.3	
Switzerland	40	6.4	
USSR	22 272	275.0	12
UK	242	55.6	230
Yugoslavia	255	23.0	
Data for the smallest states (early 1980s)			
Andorra	1	0.034	34
Monaco	0.002	0.026	13 000
San Marino	0.061	0.021	344
Vatican City State	0.004	0.001	250

Source: UN from Philips Modern School Atlas

(N.B. Due to the different sources involved, some of the figures in this table are different from those in Table 4.1.)

15 National population distributions

In all countries, people are spread unevenly. Study Figure 15.1. It shows population density in Nigeria. Concentrations of population are influenced by physical and economic factors. Medical, social and historical reasons are important too. In parts of northern and southern Nigeria mineral and agricultural resources occur. Trade links are important. Economic advantages have attracted people to these areas. The labels on Figure 15.1 show the attractions of North and South Nigeria.

Several factors have made the central belt of Nigeria unattractive to man:

1 The area has been infested with parasitic tsetse flies which cause **Trypanosomiasis** or sleeping sickness in man. The flies, or vectors since they transmit the disease, also affect domestic animals like cattle. There are many species of tsetse fly which affect animals. About five species damage man. The flies like the bushy vegetation of central Nigeria where they shade from the hot sun. The flies, about the size of our blue bottles, suck blood from man and animals. In this blood are small eel-like organisms which lie dormant in the fly. Later when the tsetse fly feeds on another creature the trypanosomes are transferred to that creature or host. The poisonous parasites grow to maturity, killing or weakening man and animals.

2 **Onchocerciasis** or river blindness is another condition caused by parasitic worms. Within twenty km of some central Nigerian rivers many people are blind through this worm (see Fig. 15.2). In this part of Africa people say 'nearness to rivers eats the eyes'.

3 Wars between tribes in central Nigeria reduced the population.

4 Slave traders from the savanna in the north and from the coast in the south captured people from this area. People were taken from these areas until the end of the nineteenth century.

5 Forest and game reserves such as Yankari east of the Jos Plateau have been made this century. They too discourage permanent settlement.

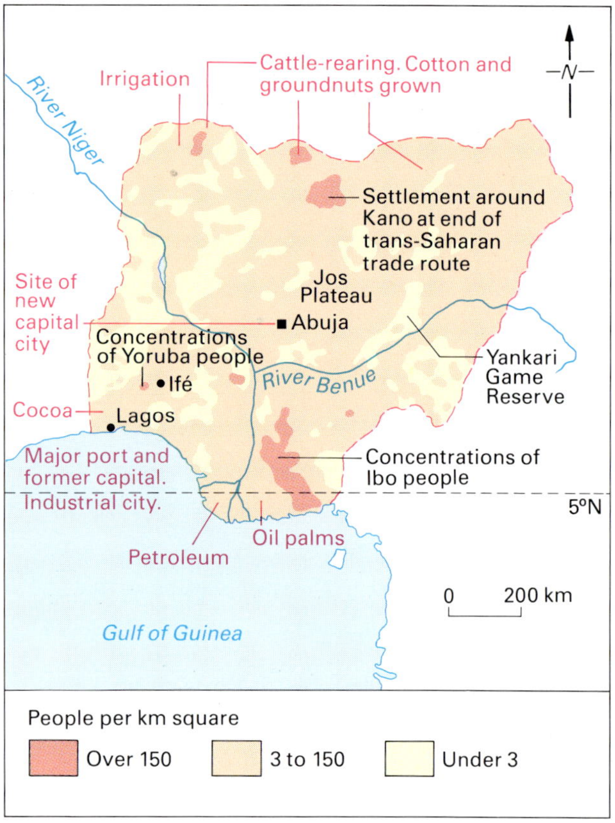

Figure 15.1 Population distribution in Nigeria.

Figure 15.2 River blindness, Nigeria

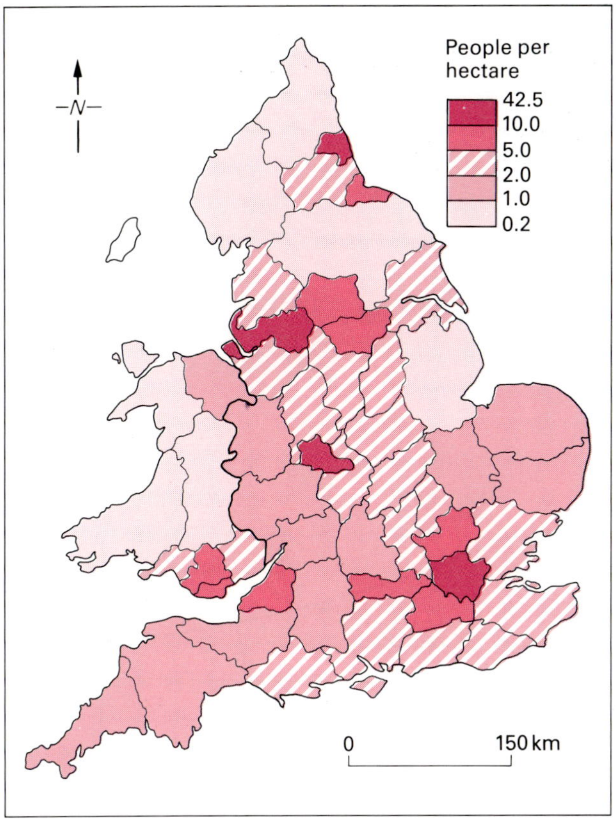

Figure 15.3 Population density in English and Welsh counties 1981.

The map in Figure 15.3 shows average population densities in English and Welsh counties in 1981. It may appear that population densities change suddenly at a county boundary. In reality changes usually occur gradually.

Figure 15.4 An area of high density population in London

You have already learnt that population is **dynamic** that means it moves and changes. Figure 15.5 maps the results of finding the **population centre** for the USA between 1790 and 1980. Gradually there has been a westward shift of the population.

Figure 15.5 The changing centre of the United States' population 1790–1980.

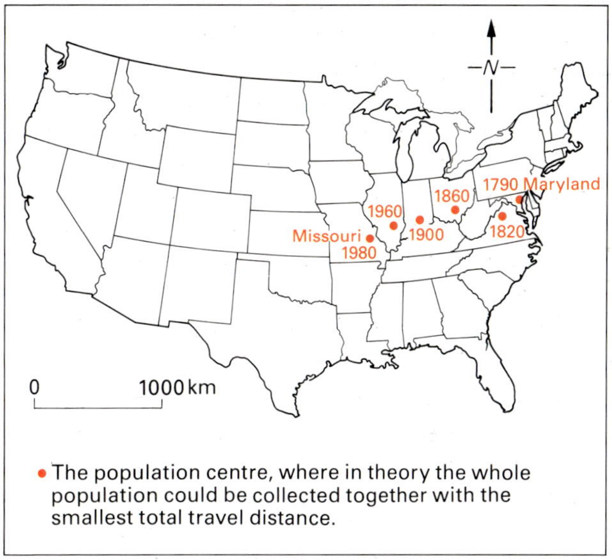

Figure 15.6 shows a **Lorenz curve**. It is a special diagram showing what percentage of the population is found on a given percentage of the land. In 1950 in the USA over sixty per cent of the population lived on about ten per cent of the area of the country. People were concentrated into clusters especially on parts of the east and west coast and near the Great Lakes.

Figure 15.6 The population concentration in the USA in 1950 shown by a Lorenz curve.

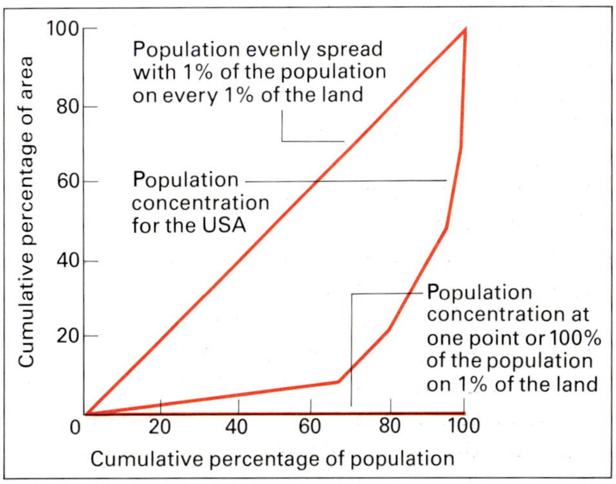

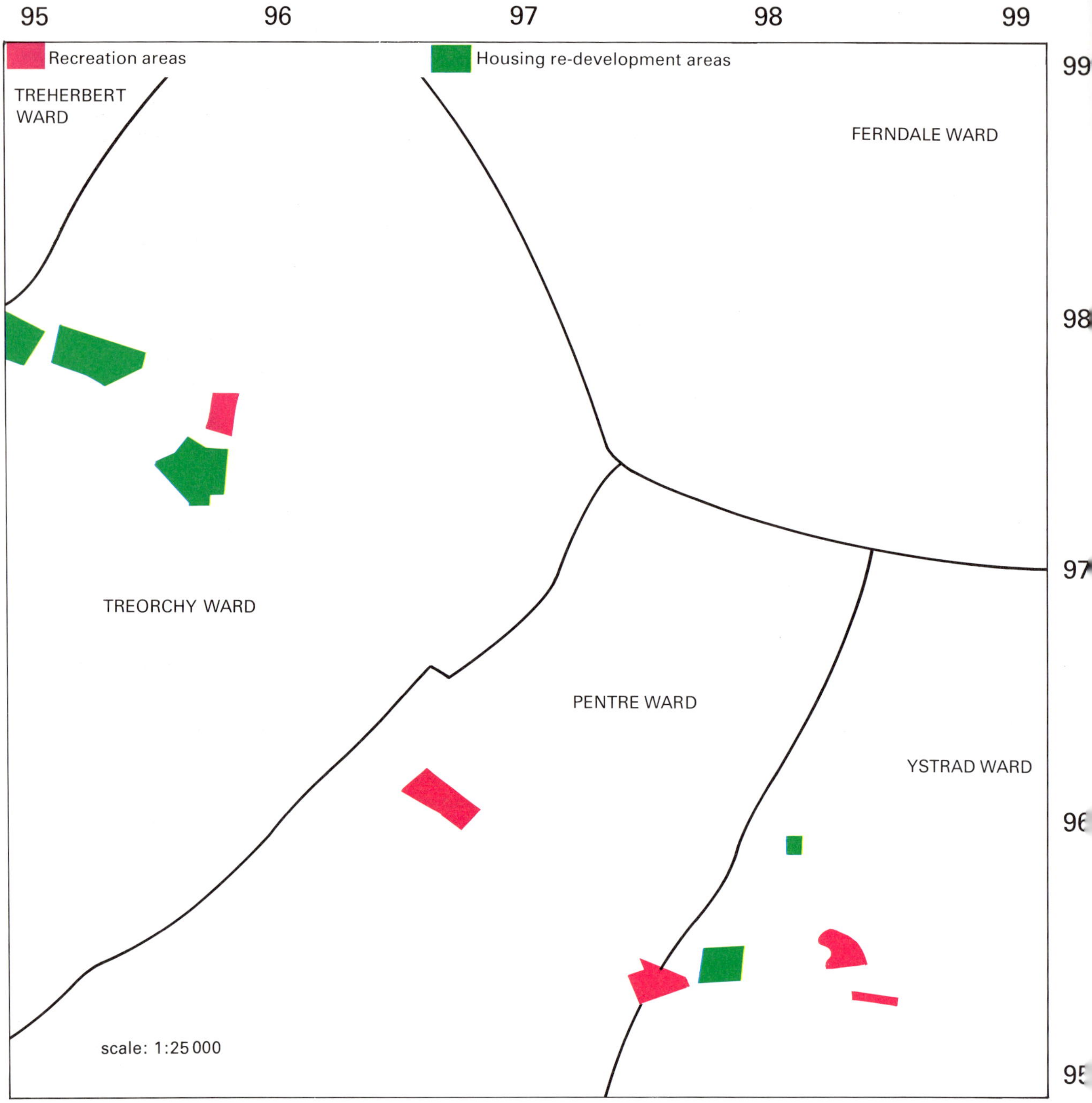

Figure 15.7 District Plan Proposals for some wards in the Rhondda Borough (pre 1984).

Table 15.1 Population changes in the wards covered by the 1:25 000 OS map extract in the Borough of the Rhondda for 1922 and 1981. (The ward boundaries were redrawn in 1984)

Ward	1922	1981
Treherbert	15 082	7450
Treorchy	17 570	7668
Pentre	12 238	5459
Ystrad	13 009	6398
Ferndale	19 360	9368

Source: Rhondda Borough Council

To find out by what percentage the population has declined in each ward from 1922 to 1981:

$$\frac{\text{1981 population for the ward}}{\text{1922 population for the ward}} \times 100$$

For example, in Treherbert Ward the population has declined to:

$$\frac{7450}{15\,082} \times 100 = 49\% \text{ of what it was in 1922}$$

The population has therefore declined by 51% since 1922.

ACTIVITIES

1 Look at Figure 15.1 (and the picture of part of Nigeria). With the help of Figure 15.1 and an atlas:

a Give five reasons why many people live in Southern Nigeria. The following list will help you:
- i Look for advantages for trade and transport.
- ii What economic resources occur there? What happens to them?
- iii What is the shape and fertility of the land like?
- iv Does the climate help farmers?

b Give as many reasons as you can why there are areas with over 150 people per square kilometre in northern Nigeria.

c What is the average density of population in central Nigeria? Give as many reasons as you can to explain why this region has low densities of people.

d What are the advantages of the location of Abuja the new Nigerian capital city?

e What are the disadvantages of Abuja's location?

2 Using Figure 15.3 and an atlas:

a Name four conurbations in England where on average population densities are over ten people per a hectare.

b Make a study of one of these urban areas to find out why people clustered in that area.

c What types of dwellings in your chosen urban area allow high densities of population to be housed?

3 Using Figure 15.3 and an atlas:

a Name all the counties in England and Wales which have less than one person per hectare on average.

b Describe the location of these counties. Do their locations have anything in common?

c Choose one county which has less than one person per hectare on average.

i Make a study of this county with the help of your atlas and books from your library. Try to find out reasons why so few people are supported by the area.
- Are there few economic resources like workable minerals?
- Is the quality of the farmland poor?
- Is there much high, steep, exposed land?
- Are communications poor?
- What is the weather like? Is it very wet? Is it very cold? Give climatic figures to support your opinions.
- Are there many jobs?
- Do young people want to live there? Are homes available?
- Is the area near a major city?

ii Make a report on your chosen county. Give the reasons why you think its average population density is low. Your report could be written; could be as a tape recording or on a wall poster.

Different groups in the class could work on different counties making different types of reports.

4 Look at Figure 15.7 of some wards in the Rhondda valley.

a On tracing paper mark the ward boundaries and the edge of the District Plan. These wards are on the Ordnance Survey extract on page 23. Place the tracing over the Ordnance Survey extract using the grid references to help you locate the wards.

Table 15.1 shows that population totals and therefore densities have declined between 1922 and 1981.

b With the help of the information on Table 15.1 work out and list for each ward by what percentage the population has declined between 1922 and 1981.

c In 1922 many people in the Rhondda valley were living in very over-crowded homes. The Medical Officer of Health reported in that year that nearly 5000 families lived in only two rooms per family. One family of twelve lived in only two rooms!

The present Rhondda District Planners want to provide housing 'better suited to the needs of the present and future population'. (see Fig. 15.8)
- i On your tracing and with the help of the Ordnance Survey extract of the Rhondda valleys, mark where you would put new houses.
- ii Mark where and what type of recreational facilities you would provide. Keep in mind the population trends, the shape of the land and the existing land use.
- iii Add to the map any other development – perhaps shops or parks which you think would improve the area.

d Explain why it is not easy to provide at once better homes and leisure facilities in an area like the Rhondda. (See Fig. 15.8.)

e Describe how population changes in some of the Rhondda valley wards have reduced some problems, but made others worse.

5 a From an atlas draw or trace a map showing the distribution of the population in the USA.

b Look at Figure 15.5. Try to find out why many people in the USA have moved westwards.

Figure 15.8 New homes in the Rhondda Valley

Coursework ideas

1 a From your school or public library or Council or Planning Office obtain a map of the wards – or some wards – in your town or nearest town. You may have to make a tracing from a borrowed map.
  b Find out the population in a recent year for each ward. Find out the population for the same wards ten, twenty or more years ago. Calculate, as in Table 15.1, the percentage population change.
  c Visit the areas concerned. Observe, map and record, using sketches or photographs the effects of population change on the area.

2 Conduct local field work to see if different ages of housing have different densities.
  a Walk through the settlement recording on a map where different styles and ages of homes occur.
  b On a larger scale map of your town rule lightly in pencil small squares of equal size. Draw the squares – perhaps of one centimetre square for a 1:25 000 scale Ordnance Survey map – where you know different ages of homes are found. Go to those areas and count the number of homes or separate dwellings found there. Record the information.
  c Transfer the results of your investigation into a report. Explain fully how you collected your information. Use maps, sketches and other illustrations to help you reach your conclusion.

3 Test the hypothesis that fewer dwellings are found on higher land, steeper slopes or shaded slopes.
  a Select a suitable area for your study such as across a valley. Draw a transect or cross-section of the area from a large-scale Ordnance Survey map or make your own transect. (Your teacher will be able to help explain how you can do this.) Make sure you take a line across land you may walk over or can see.
  b Following the transect record on it the location of numbers and types of dwellings.
  c Consider what factors, other than physical geography, may account for your observations.

16 The nature and causes of migration

Perhaps you have lived in more than one place since you were born. Possibly you have had to travel to school. You may have travelled further on holiday. All these movements are called **migrations** and are of interest to a geographer. Look at Figure 16.1. It shows why some people moved recently.

Permanent migration involves people moving for good to a new area (see Fig. 16.2). Sometimes the new area is in another country or continent. **Temporary migration** is when people move from one place to another for a short time. They usually return home.

Figure 16.1 Causes of migration

TAMIL refugees seeking asylum in Britain claim they are persecuted in Sri Lanka.

Ethiopia's Marxist Government estimates the drought has affected life for 7.7 million people in this country of 33 million, forcing 2.2 million from their homes and threatening 5.5 million with starvation.

LEIGH offers to success oriented individuals, a career opportunity in Canada's high technology growth industry coupled with competitive salaries, excellent benefits and a comprehensive "Relocation to Canada" package.

Houses crushed

A landslip in the north-west Yugoslav mining town of Zagorje ob Savi destroyed eight houses and a factory. Residents and machinery had been evacuated. —Reuter.

RETIRE IN STYLE

From £46,850. Fabulous Regency-style cottages and apartments purpose built for perfect retirement in elegant Cheltenham.

They have fled in fear from widespread fighting between Government and rebel forces. The rebels of the Mozambique National Resistance (MNR) are burning villages, destroying schools and health posts, and making it unsafe to use roads or grow food in many areas.

Pozzuoli has the rare distinction of being founded on the roof of a volcano. The worst, and most recent, disturbance ended in January 1985, after 18 months in which a bulge, 1·8 metres high at its peak, appeared over some 80 square kilometres. In Pozzuoli, sitting astride the developing summit, the immediate repercussions were ruinous: of the town's 72,000 inhabitants, over half were obliged to abandon homes made unsafe by the movement of the ground. As the sheltered harbour became shallower, so more and more of the local fishing fleet had to find anchorage elsewhere. Tourism slumped.

Figure 16.2 War time refugees

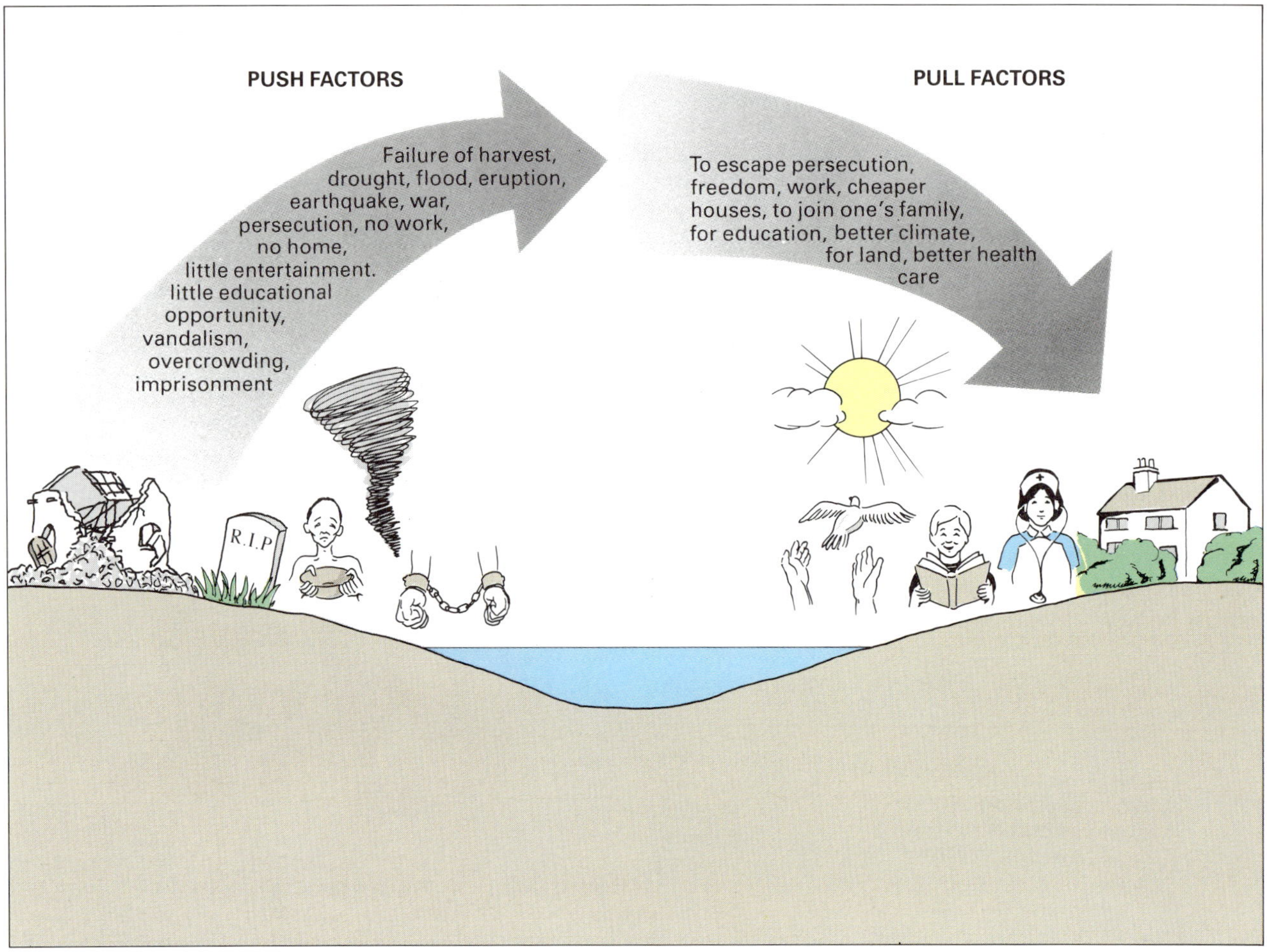

Figure 16.3 Push and pull factors on where to live.

There are two sets of reasons which often combine to explain migrations. They are called **push** and **pull factors**. Push factors force people from an area. Pull factors attract people to an area. Figure 16.3 shows some push and pull factors.

ACTIVITIES

1 Look at Figure 16.1. Make two lists, one giving examples of 'pull' factors and the other examples of 'push' factors. Try to add more of your own.

2 a On two maps of the world use Table 16.1 to draw arrows to show the direction of migration to and from the United Kingdom recently.
You could make the width of the arrows proportional to the number of migrants.
Use one map to show the number and origin of people entering Britain. On the other map show the number and destination of migrants leaving Britain. Give your maps titles and keys.

b Where do most immigrants come from? Why?

Table 16.1 The origin and numbers of migrants to and from the United Kingdom – mid 1985–mid 1986

Country of last or next place of residence	Numbers entering the UK in thousands	Numbers leaving the UK in thousands
Commonwealth countries		
Australia	16	23
Canada	4	6
New Zealand	7	8
African countries	13	6
Bangladesh, India, Sri Lanka	15	3
Caribbean	5	2
Other Commonwealth countries	20	15
Non-Commonwealth countries		
European Community	55	33
Rest of Europe	18	17
United States of America	25	27
Other American countries	2	4
Republic of South Africa	19	3
Pakistan	10	2
Middle East	16	17
Other Foreign countries	16	10

Source: OPCS Monitor MN 87/3 1987

17 *Permanent migration*

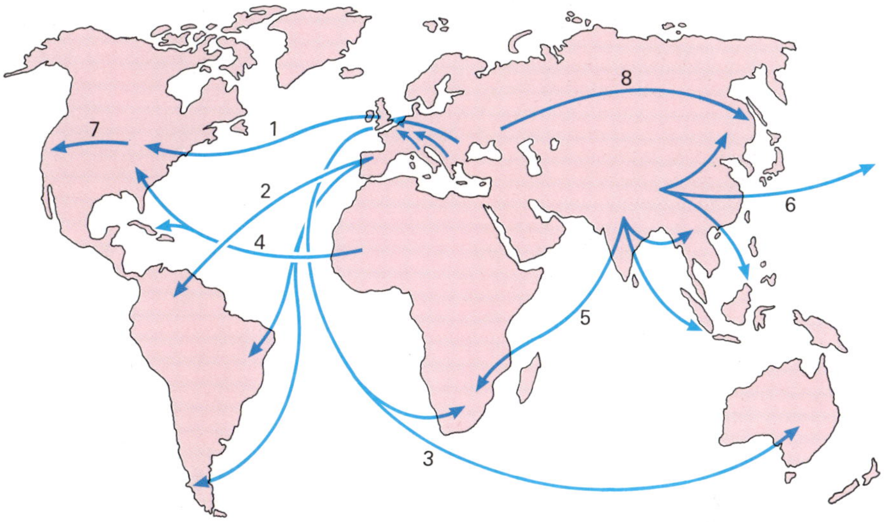

Figure 17.1 Major intercontinental migration from the sixteenth century on. See Figure 17.5 also.

Moving to a new place permanently may be very disturbing even if people move willingly. Much has to be arranged even to move a short distance from one home to another in the same town. At times, large numbers of people have been involved in major migrations. They may have gone overseas or to completely strange areas. Sometimes they have been moved against their will. Look at Figure 17.1 which shows some intercontinental movement from the sixteenth century.

During the Second World War, 1939–1945, about twenty-five million people migrated. Some moved as refugees away from invaded or battle areas (Fig. 16.2). Some were put in concentration camps. Some were soldiers or prisoners. After the war over fourteen million people moved into West Germany from lands to the east. In 1961 the Berlin Wall was built to stop people from East Germany escaping to the West (see Fig. 17.2).

Israel since its foundation in 1948 has received immigrants from seventy countries. The Law of Return grants every Jew the right to settle there and become an Israeli citizen. The population of 806 thousand in 1948 has increased to 4.3 million. 1.4 million of these have been migrants with about half from Europe and the Americas.

Figure 17.2 The Berlin Wall

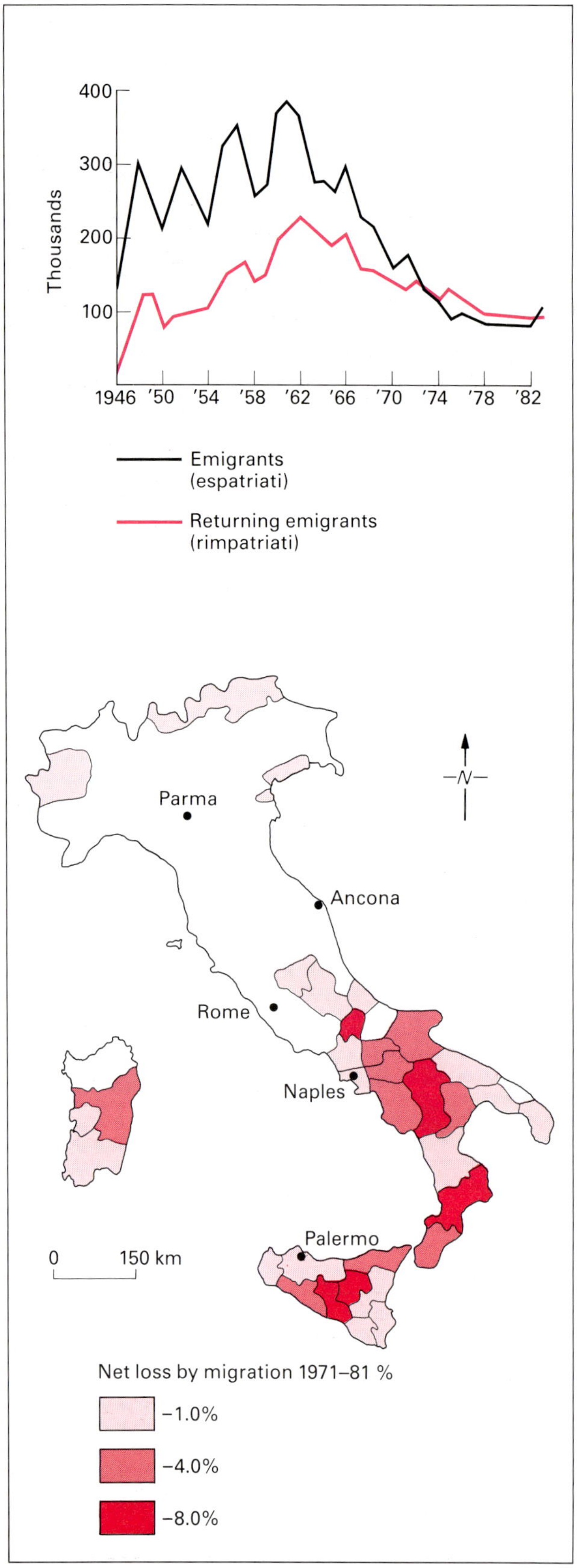

Figure 17.4 Impoverished Southern Italy

In 1961, 113 000 Commonwealth immigrants mainly from the Caribbean came to the United Kingdom to work or to join their families.

Look at Figure 17.3. It shows that people have left some northern and many southern provinces in Italy (see Fig. 17.4). It has been estimated that twenty-six million Italians have emigrated since 1860.

Permanent migration also occurs within countries like Italy and the United Kingdom. A recent trend in many large European cities such as London has been a loss of population, particularly from central areas. People have been moving from **urban** to **rural** areas. Interestingly, however, in the three years between 1984 and 1987 Greater London showed a slight increase in total population.

In Norway in recent years there has been a shift in population especially from the northern counties in the Arctic. Look at Figure 17.10. Norwegians have been moving to the more southerly counties near Oslo, the capital.

Figure 17.3 Italian migration 1946–1982.

Figure 17.5 Migrating to North America from Ireland in the mid-nineteenth century

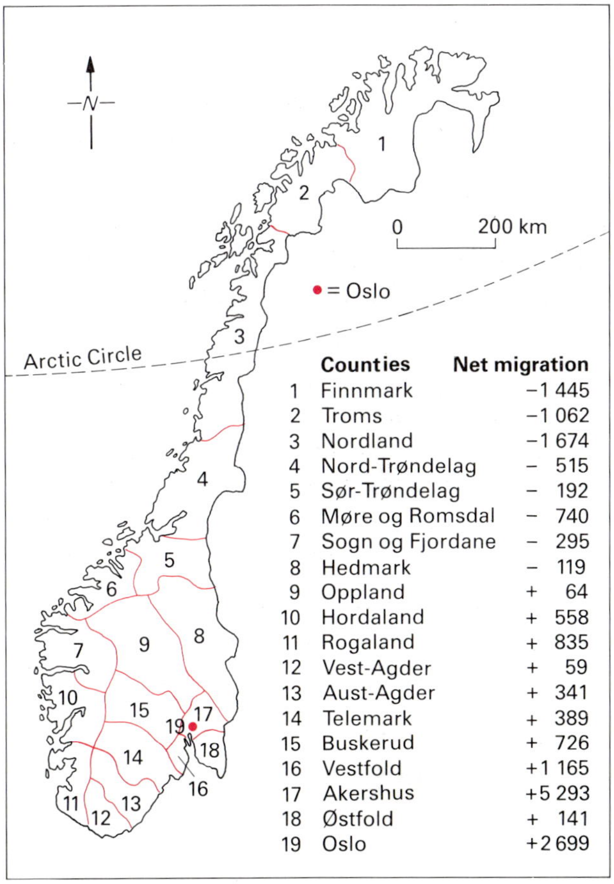

	Counties	Net migration
1	Finnmark	−1 445
2	Troms	−1 062
3	Nordland	−1 674
4	Nord-Trøndelag	− 515
5	Sør-Trøndelag	− 192
6	Møre og Romsdal	− 740
7	Sogn og Fjordane	− 295
8	Hedmark	− 119
9	Oppland	+ 64
10	Hordaland	+ 558
11	Rogaland	+ 835
12	Vest-Agder	+ 59
13	Aust-Agder	+ 341
14	Telemark	+ 389
15	Buskerud	+ 726
16	Vestfold	+1 165
17	Akershus	+5 293
18	Østfold	+ 141
19	Oslo	+2 699

Figure 17.10 Population movement by migration in Norwegian counties in 1985.

ACTIVITIES

1 On an outline map of the world, mark the major migrations since the sixteenth century and add examples of recent migrations described in this section or known by your class.

2 Trace a large-scale map of North America. Using an Atlas, on your map:

a mark all settlements named after places in Britain in one colour;

b mark all settlements named after places in France in another colour;

c mark all settlements named after places in Spain in another colour;

d which parts of North America were settled by British, French and Spanish migrants?

3 a Trace the map of Italy in Figure 17.3 showing areas of **out-migration**. With the help of information in an atlas, label your tracing to describe the nature of the physical geography of the areas losing population.

b Read Figure 17.6. List the main reasons why many people have left southern Italy. Where have they gone?

c What do you think could be done, if anything, to help people stay in southern Italy?

d Try to find out from your library what improvement schemes have been introduced in southern Italy since 1950.

Rich and poor: Tale of two countries

David Willey

Despite the pouring of thousands of millions of pounds of taxpayers' money into the economically less developed South during the past 40 years to implant new industries and to improve communications, the image of two Italys — the go-ahead North and the backward South — seems more, not less real. Although the citizens of Palermo and the citizens of Parma may watch the same television programmes, and go to the polls on the same day, they are living in different worlds.

While the big cities of northern Italy, and smaller wealth-generating industrial centres in the North like Parma forge ahead, achieving living standards for many Italians that exceed those of their social counterparts in Britain, the South remains stuck with ancient and apparently insoluble problems.

The imbalance shows up in practically all the statistics, beginning with the key index, unemployment. Whereas the overall percentage of unemployed for the whole of Italy in 1987 is 12 per cent, the figure for the South rises to 20 per cent, while in the North it falls to 7.5 per cent.

The main reason for the chronic lack of jobs in the South is the lack of industry; 80 per cent of Italian heavy and light industry is located in the North. Six per cent of southerners are still classified as illiterate, in comparison with only just over 1 per cent in the centre and North.

Consumer statistics point up gaps in living standards. In Calabria, family spending is 30 per cent below the national average. Calabrians own fewer cars, fewer television sets, make fewer calls from fewer telephones.

In prosperous Lombardy the local per capita gross product is 130 per cent above that of the Calabrian worker. A Milanese worker can afford to dress better, eat more expensive foods, can go out more often to sporting events, theatre, cinema or discos.

In the South, jobs in the public sector are regarded as pure gold for, once obtained, they offer security for life. So public competitions for even humble posts as janitors or secretaries attract many thousands of applicants and are fought with the powerful weapon of recommendations — letters of support from politicians or bishops or civil servants, the higher ranking the better.

Although Italians are marrying less and having fewer children (the population has actually begun to decline), the demographic picture varies radically between North and South. Southerners have an average two or three children, while the typical family in the North has one child. Divorce and abortion, which are both now legal in Italy, are practised much more in the North than in the more Catholic and traditionally minded South.

In Naples the family remains virtually the only stabilising force in a society which is falling apart at the seams through increasing drug addiction, organised crime and administrative neglect. The taps in the biggest city in southern Italy frequently run dry. Two thousand crimes of violence are reported each day to the police.

The family simply has to fill in where the State or local government fails. There is growing political disaffection in the South.

The North-South gap remains stubbornly there, and seems destined to grow.

The *Observer* 15.11.87

Figure 17.6

ACTIVITIES

4 Read Figure 17.7 and with the help of Figure 17.8 describe and attempt to explain the direction of migration of population in the United Kingdom since 1971.

Exodus in search of 'good life'

AN INCREASING number of people are deserting Britain's cities in search of a more relaxed lifestyle in the country.

The exodus, particularly from London, now far exceeds the trend of rural depopulation in many areas, research findings show.

David Cross, of King's College London, used census information and the Registrar General's annual estimates of population to determine how much of the population growth in rural areas is due to long distance migration.

Of the 529 000 rise in population between 1971 and 1986 in the "top 33" rural growth areas, 97 per cent was due to migration, Mr Cross said.

And between 60 and 70 per cent of the gains were due to long distance migration between regions.

Leading the list of favourite destinations were: Wimborne, Dorset; Huntington; Caradon, near Plymouth; north Cornwall; Radnor in mid Wales; Forest Heath and Babergh in Suffolk; Breckland in Norfolk; Ryedale and Selby in north Yorkshire; east Yorkshire; and Holderness in Humberside.

The main trend, Mr Cross told the conference, was that while the more remote rural areas were often losing population through natural change as old people died and young people left to find work in the cities, this was being far outstripped by the new gains.

And more than a quarter of the new arrivals were in the 15 to 29 key worker age group.

Mr Cross said the reasons for the exodus included an increasing deconcentration of employment opportunities, improvement of travel facilities – particularly the high-speed rail links between East Anglia and London – and high property prices in London which enabled people to sell their homes at a large profit and move out.

The *Independent* 8.1.88

Figure 17.7

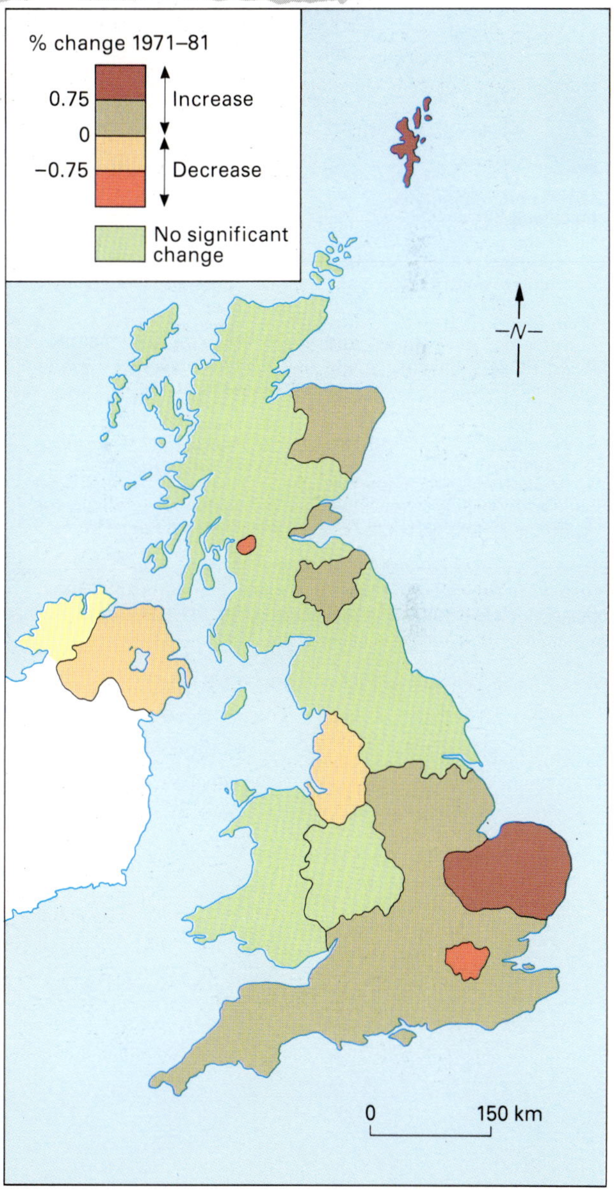

Figure 17.8 Population change in the UK 1971–1981 through migration.

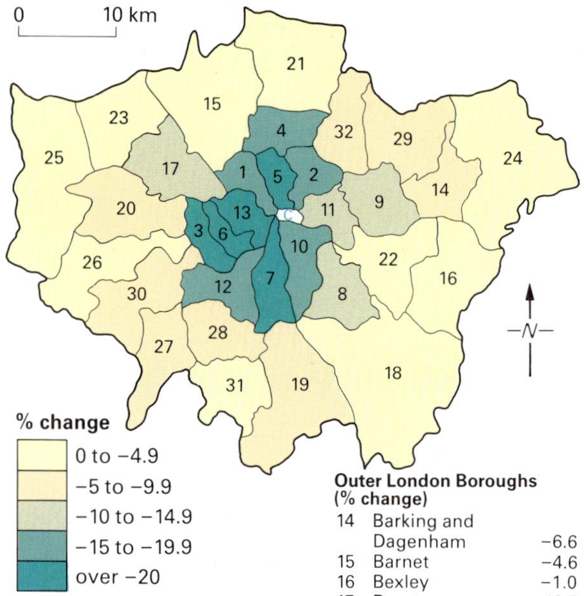

Inner London Boroughs (% change)

1	Camden	−17.0
2	Hackney	−18.2
3	Hammersmith & Fulham	−20.9
4	Haringey	−15.4
5	Islington	−20.9
6	Kensington and Chelsea	−26.3
7	Lambeth	−20.1
8	Lewisham	−13.1
9	Newham	−11.8
10	Southwark	−19.2
11	Tower Hamlets	−13.8
12	Wandsworth	−15.4
13	City of Westminster	−20.5

Outer London Boroughs (% change)

14	Barking and Dagenham	−6.6
15	Barnet	−4.6
16	Bexley	−1.0
17	Brent	−10.5
18	Bromley	−3.6
19	Croydon	−5.2
20	Ealing	−7.0
21	Enfield	−3.4
22	Greenwich	−2.7
23	Harrow	−3.6
24	Havering	−3.0
25	Hillingdon	−2.4
26	Hounslow	−3.5
27	Kingston-upon-Thames	−5.8
28	Merton	−7.0
29	Redbridge	−6.2
30	Richmond-upon-Thames	−9.6
31	Sutton	−0.6
32	Waltham Forest	−8.3

C = The City

Figure 17.9 Population change in Greater London 1971–1981. Population total 6 696 008 – declined by 10.1% from 1971.

ACTIVITIES

5 a Make a tracing of Figure 17.9 which shows the Boroughs of Greater London. Use your own colour scheme to shade each borough according to its population change. The groups are:

Boroughs showing	0 to −4.9%	population	change	or loss
	−5 to −9.9%	"	"	"
	−10 to −14.9%	"	"	"
	−15 to −19.9%	"	"	"
	−20% or more	"	"	"

Remember to use the darkest shade for the over −20% category.

b Describe the map. Which areas lost most people? Discuss as a class what the reasons for this might be.

c Make a collection of estate agents' descriptions of similar houses for sale in different parts of London from a national newspaper – weekend papers often have a selection. Where are houses most expensive? Try to explain this.

d As a class, make a wall display of current newspaper cuttings about London. Do this for a month. At the end of that time what items have been featured? Which of the items help explain why people are moving from Greater London?

e How has the redevelopment of London Docklands encouraged people to move recently – especially since 1984 – into some Inner London Boroughs like Tower Hamlets? (Inner city redevelopment is dealt with in the *Settlement* book.)

6 a Trace the counties of Norway from Figure 17.10.

i Shade in one colour areas which have lost population and in another colour counties which have gained population.

ii Make a key. Give the map a title.

b Using your atlas and your library, find out what the weather and length of daylight are like north of the Arctic Circle in Norway in January. In what way are conditions in Oslo different?

c From your atlas count the number of towns in Arctic Norway. Are there many **central places** providing high order goods and services?

d Describe what your atlas shows about the type and direction of communications in Finnmark, Troms and Nordland in Norway.

e Write a short report suggesting reasons why many people choose not to live in Arctic Norway.

f From your atlas look at the countries which border Norway in the Arctic Circle. Why are the Norwegian Government and NATO members keen that the region remains populated?

g Imagine you are a Norwegian Government minister responsible for stopping out-migration in Arctic Norway. Outline, in a brief report, what the Government could do to attract more people to the area.

18 Case study: Migration in Indonesia

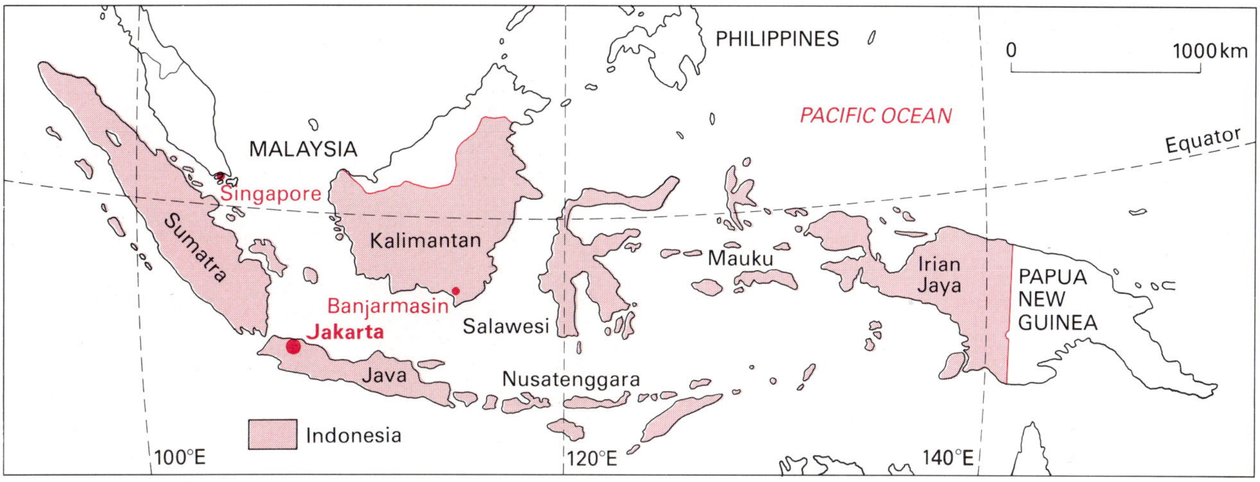

Figure 18.1 Indonesia

Table 18.1 Population distribution in Indonesia 1985 (estimated)

Province or island	Area in km^2	Population in 000s	% of Indonesia's population	Population density per km^2
Sumatra	473 606	32 922	19.93	70
Java	132 187	100 279	60.72	759
Nusatenggara (Bali, West Nusatenggara, East Nusatenggara, East Timor)	88 488	9411	5.70	106
Kalimantan	539 460	7842	4.75	15
Sulawesi	189 216	11 688	7.08	62
Maluku	74 505	1646	0.99	22
Irian Jaya	421 981	1368	0.83	3

Source: *Facts on Transmigration* Dept. of Information, Rep. of Indonesia

Indonesia consists of nearly 14 000 tropical islands in the west of the Pacific Ocean between Malaysia and Australia. Figure 18.1 shows the location of the main islands and of Jakarta, the capital.

The estimated population of Indonesia in 1986 was 169 million. Look at Table 18.1. Compare the population distribution on the principal islands. Population distribution is very uneven in Indonesia. Over sixty per cent of the people live on Java (see Fig. 18.2).

Figure 18.2 Squatter homes of rural to urban migrants in Jakarta

Two types of permanent migrations are occurring in Indonesia. Firstly, many people are moving from **rural to urban** areas like Jakarta. In 1971 eighty-three per cent of Idonesians lived in the countryside with only seventeen per cent in urban areas. By 1980, the percentage of urban dwellers had risen to twenty-two per cent. Migration as well as a high birth-rate account for this increase.

Secondly, since 1905 there has been Government sponsored **transmigration**. This involves the voluntary resettlement of families from the over-populated islands with high unemployment like Java to islands like Sumatra, Kalimantan, Sulawesi and Irian Jaya. These islands have plenty of land and need labour for development. Figure 18.3 shows the numbers of families who have moved in successive five-year plans (see Fig. 18.4).

Iskani is a fifty year old farmer. He moved with his parents to one of sixty-three transmigration sites at Takisung near Banjarmasin on Kalimantan. They moved from east Java in 1953. At first the Government only cleared the land. They did not offer expert guidance or fertilizers for the poor soil. It took all day on bad roads to get to market. Now, schools, a health centre, mosques and better roads serve the residents.

More recently the Government has provided each migrant family with at least two hectares of land. They are given a two room house and help in obtaining tools, seeds and seedlings of cash crops like coconuts, cloves and coffee.

Sukarman went to Kalimantan from east Java in 1986. On Java he owned 25 m^2 on which his house stood and his family income was about £15 a month. He has prospered from transmigration. He now owns 25 ha of land and his monthly income is over £30 a month.

With the help of funds from the World Bank, Indonesia has built health centres, schools, roads and sugar mills in the reclaimed areas of settlement. It is feared, however, that new transmigration schemes will slacken. This is because the price for Indonesia's oil fell on world markets in 1986. The Government has had to cut the budget for transmigration by fifty-four per cent. Indonesia will now improve areas already settled.

Some people would welcome less transmigration. They believe it destroys the lives of tribal people, damages fragile forest environments and does nothing to reduce the high birth rate on Java.

Figure 18.4 Transmigrants on Kalimantan

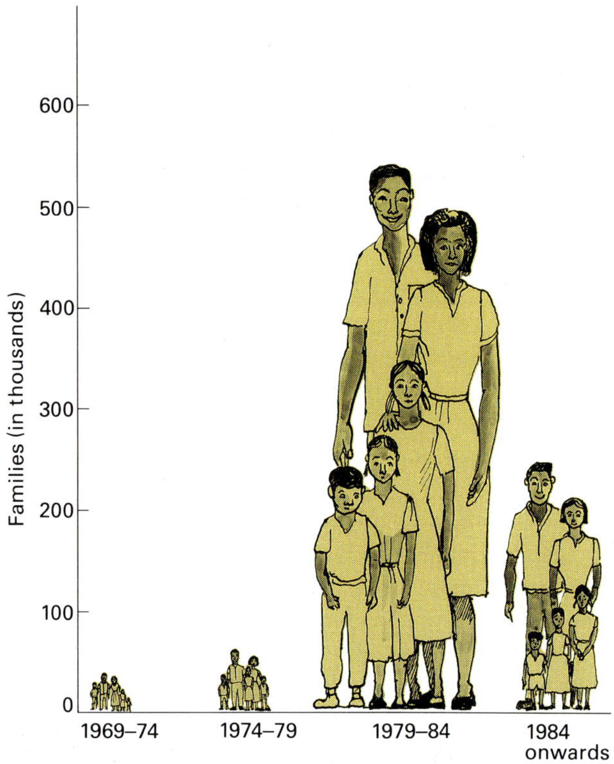

Figure 18.3 Numbers of transmigrant families in Indonesia in successive five-year plans.

Figure 18.5 A satellite image of part of Java. Blue and black indicates water; pale green indicates limestone; green indicates rice growing; pink shows tea growing; the central green area is the Bandung Plain surrounded by volcanoes; dark red indicates very thick vegetation.

ACTIVITIES

1 Draw a map of Indonesia from Figure 18.1. Use information in the text to show by arrows the direction of the two types of migration in the country. Use different colours for each type of migration.

2 a Draw a bar chart to show the population of each province or main island in Indonesia from Table 18.1.

b From Table 18.1 write down the Indonesian island with the largest population and give its population density.

c Which two islands have the lowest population densities?

d What does transmigration try to do?

3 Look at the photograph of the home and land of a transmigrant in Kalimantan (Figure 18.4).

i Draw a labelled sketch of the picture. Your labels need to show the style of the house; what it is made of; why the roof overhangs the walls and why it has shutters.

ii Add labels describing the use of the surrounding land.

4 a Draw a climatic graph for Indonesia using the following figures:

	J	F	M	A	M	J	J	A	S	O	N	D	
Temperature °C	26	26	26	27	27	26	26	26	27	27	26	26	Average 26
Rainfall in cm	30	30	21	15	11	10	6	4	7	11	14	20	Total for year 179 cm

b In what way does the climate influence:

i the style and building materials of the houses of transmigrants?

ii the crops grown by transmigrants?

5 Draw a pie-chart or pie-diagram from Table 18.1 to show what percentage of Indonesia's population live in each area shown in Figure 18.1. (To find the number of degrees, multiply the percentage figures by 3.6.)

6 Look at the satellite image of part of Java. (Fig. 18.5)

a What natural hazard could affect the area?

b How can the products of this hazard prove valuable to farmers?

c What protects the soil from erosion by the tropical rains?

d Does the image confirm your knowledge that Java is one of the most densely populated islands in the world?

19 *Temporary migration*

Journeys to and from work and on holiday are examples of **temporary migration**.

The journey to work

In Britain many people have chosen to live away from their jobs. More and more people now live on the fringe of urban areas or in villages and **commute** daily to the cities. Increasing car ownership since the 1960s has been largely to blame for this trend. Read Figure 17.7 to discover which rural areas in England and Wales are gaining most people.

Improved rail services through electrification to London has encouraged the growth of commuting (see Fig. 19.1). Electrification can be said to reduce the **friction of distance** (see Table 19.1). Overcrowded roads and trains occur because many people travel to work at the same time.

Figure 19.1 Weekday commuting to London

In the north east of England, the Tyne and Wear Integrated Transport Network was opened in 1984. It was built to improve public transport in an area where forty per cent of households were without cars. Look at Figure 19.2 which shows the network.

Figure 19.2 The area served by the Tyne and Wear Integrated Public Transport System.

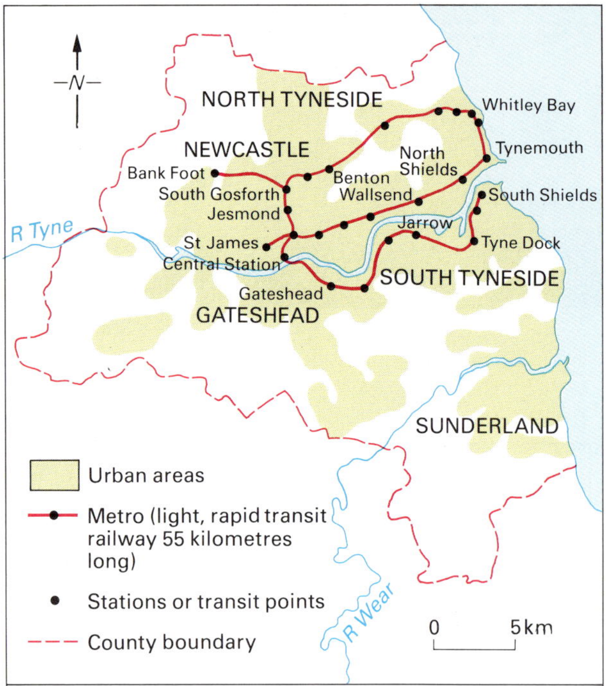

Metro-related travel time savings on public transport

Journeys between centres	Savings in minutes
Bankfoot – South Shields area	35
Regent Centre – Jarrow and South Shields area	20
Team Valley – North Shields area	20
Gateshead – Metro areas North of River Tyne	10–20
Sunderland – Metro areas North of River Tyne	8–10
Washington – Metro areas North of River Tyne	20–30
South Shields – West Newcastle	13–19
South Shields – Gateshead	15
South Shields – Sunderland	0
North Shields – Gateshead area	7–20

Light, rapid, metro trains carry commuters from housing estates to work on new industrial estates on the edge of the city (see Fig. 19.3). Passengers travel in to the centre of the city for work, shopping and entertainment. Buses are timed to fit in with the arrival and departure of trains. Tickets can be used on buses or trains throughout the network.

Within Western Europe many people migrate long distances to find work. They may remain away from home for weeks or months or even years. Many unskilled workers left Italy, Yugoslavia and Turkey in the 1960s and 1970s to seek work in richer countries like West Germany and Switzerland (see Fig. 19.4).

In Nigeria young men in their twenties helped build a new University at Ife in 1967. People now move to the University for study and to help run it.

Figure 19.5 A migrant worker in Africa

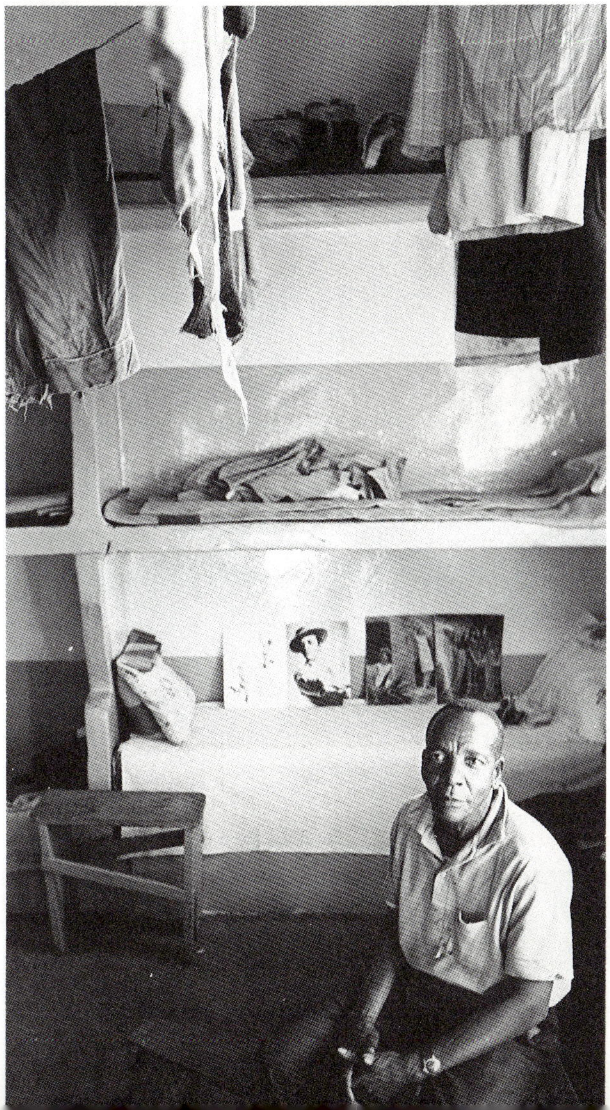

Figure 19.3 The Tyne and Wear Metro System

Figure 19.4 Turkish migrant workers in West Germany

Black workers are employed in South African gold mines. Many men migrate for a year from neighbouring states like Botswana. While away from home they live in hostel accommodation. In 1982–83 1.4 million black migrants worked in the gold mines. Up to two million non-whites have migrated to squatter settlements on the outskirts of cities like Cape Town seeking work (see Fig. 19.5).

Traditionally pastoral farmers in countries like Norway, France and Nigeria have migrated seasonally with their livestock. This involves the movement to fresh pastures and is called **transhumance**.

Holidays

In the developed countries of the western world the number of people who travel on holiday has increased this century. They can do this because:

1 workers have paid holidays;
2 they can afford to travel;
3 they have time to travel;
4 they are interested in seeing or being in another place where the scenery, climate and way of life may be different;
5 there are good communications by road, rail, sea and air links. Increasingly people are travelling abroad.

Figure 19.8 European and North

Figure 19.7 Package holiday ma
Majorca.

Figure 19.6
Day trippers at the seaside in Cornwall

sts in the Caribbean

Palma Airport,

In Britain there are three types of tourist; the foreign tourist; the day-tripper (see Fig. 19.6) and the tourist who spends some days or weeks in one resort (see Fig. 19.7).

Increasingly people from the developed world are holidaying further afield in developing countries. For example, British and American tourists visit Caribbean islands like Barbados to escape the winter cold (see Fig. 19.8). People travel for beach holidays to countries like the Gambia or to see historical monuments like the pyramids in Egypt. Some go on safari in Kenya or to make treks in the Himalayas. It is fast air travel, often in specially chartered 'planes, which allows more people to go further in a shorter time.

Travel can help people to learn more of the world and gain a better understanding of problems and issues facing us all. (The tourist industry is covered in the *Energy and Industry* book.)

ACTIVITIES

1 a Trace the true distance diagram showing British Rail stations between London and Peterborough from Figure 19.9. Beside it, using the time distances from Table 19.1 and the given time scale, plot the journey times along the same route.

b Which stations have been brought relatively closer to London? What effect may this have on commuting?

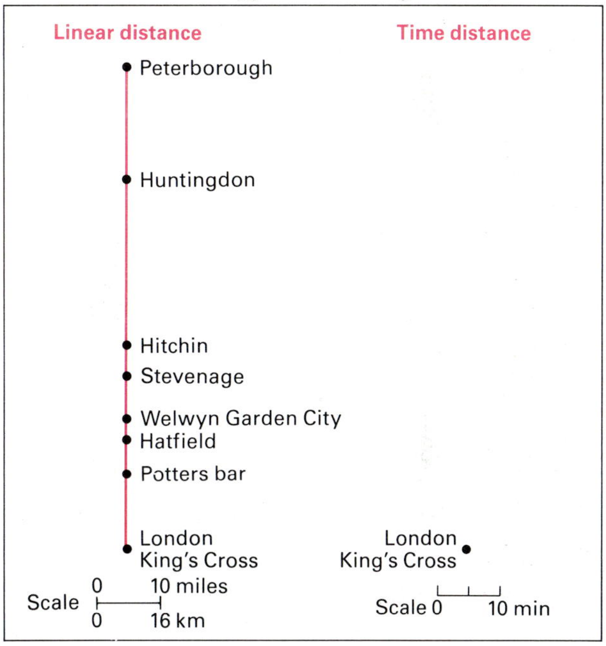

Figure 19.9 A comparison between the relative linear and time distance by rail between Peterborough and London.

Table 19.1 Shortest weekday rail journey time between Peterborough and London, Kings' Cross

From	Linear distance to London, King's Cross Miles	Kilometres	Time distance to London, Kings' Cross Minutes
Peterborough	76.25	122	57
Huntingdon	58.75	94	47
Hitchin	32	51.2	29
Stevenage	27.5	44	26
Welwyn Garden City	20.25	32.4	25
Hatfield	17.25	27.6	22
Potters Bar	12.25	19.6	16

Source: British Rail Timetable

ACTIVITIES

2 a Look at Figure 19.2 of the Tyne and Wear Integrated Transport System. In what way has it helped someone living in Bank Foot and working in South Shields?

b What are the benefits to the traveller of co-ordinating bus and train services and fares?

c Look at Figure 19.10. When are the peak travel times during a weekday? Who uses the network then? When are peak times on Saturday? Who uses the network then?

3 a On a copy of the map of Europe (one is in the *Teachers' Book*) use the data in Table 19.2 to draw arrows to plot the flow of migrant workers to the Federal Republic of Germany (West Germany) in 1982 from other European countries. Make a scale so you can draw arrows of different thickness according to the number of migrants.

b Study the figures for 1974. Describe the trend in migrants from 1974 to 1982. Try to account for it.

4 Study the population pyramids of immigrant workers to France in 1974 and 1980 shown in Figure 19.11.

a What are the two age groups most immigrants fit into? Why do you think this is so?

b Why do you think there are so few migrants aged over forty?

c Describe and try to account for the major differences between the two pyramids.

d Construct a bar chart to show the information given in Table 19.3.

e Under the title 'Immigration to France' use the work you have completed to write a few summary points.

Figure 19.10 Metro boardings weekdays and Saturdays May 1984 on the Tyne and Wear Integrated Transport System.

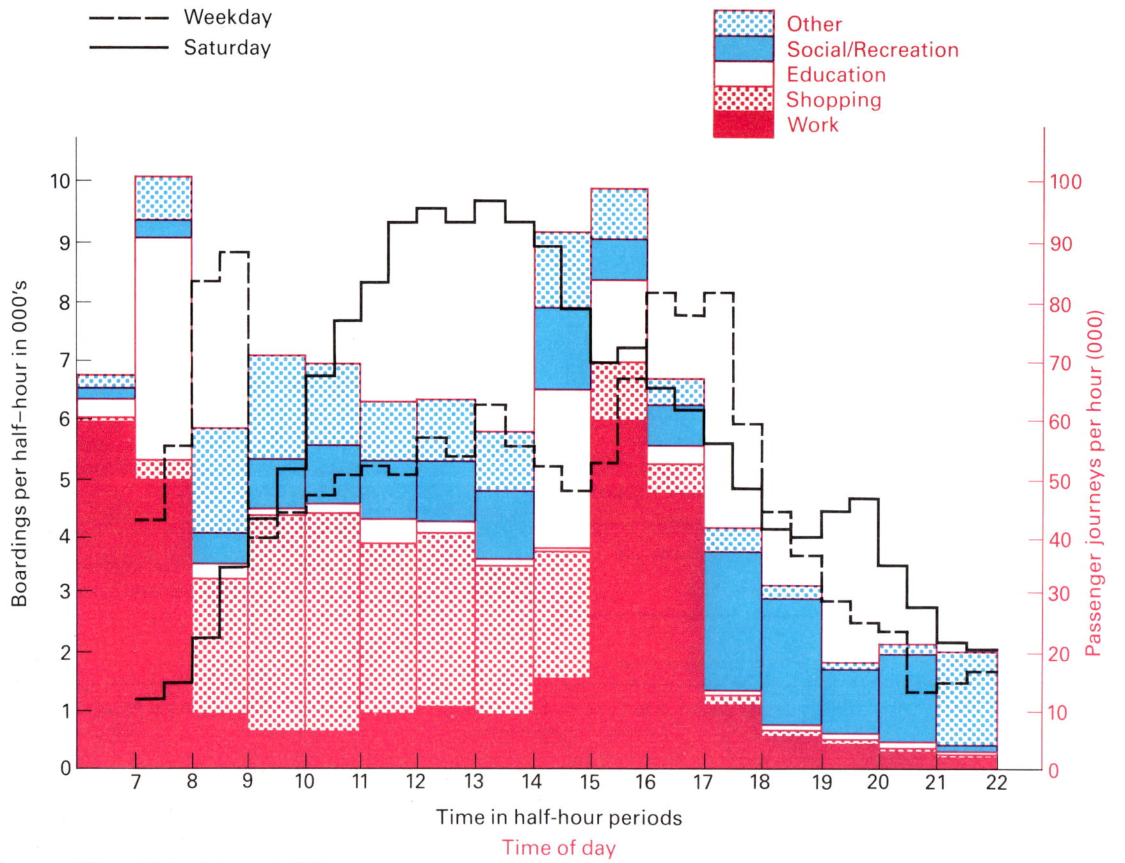

The Tyne and Wear Metro Integrated System fulfils a broad diversity of travel needs, for social and leisure purposes as well as work. (The Metro Report)

Public transport journeys by purpose and time or day (weekday 1984/85)

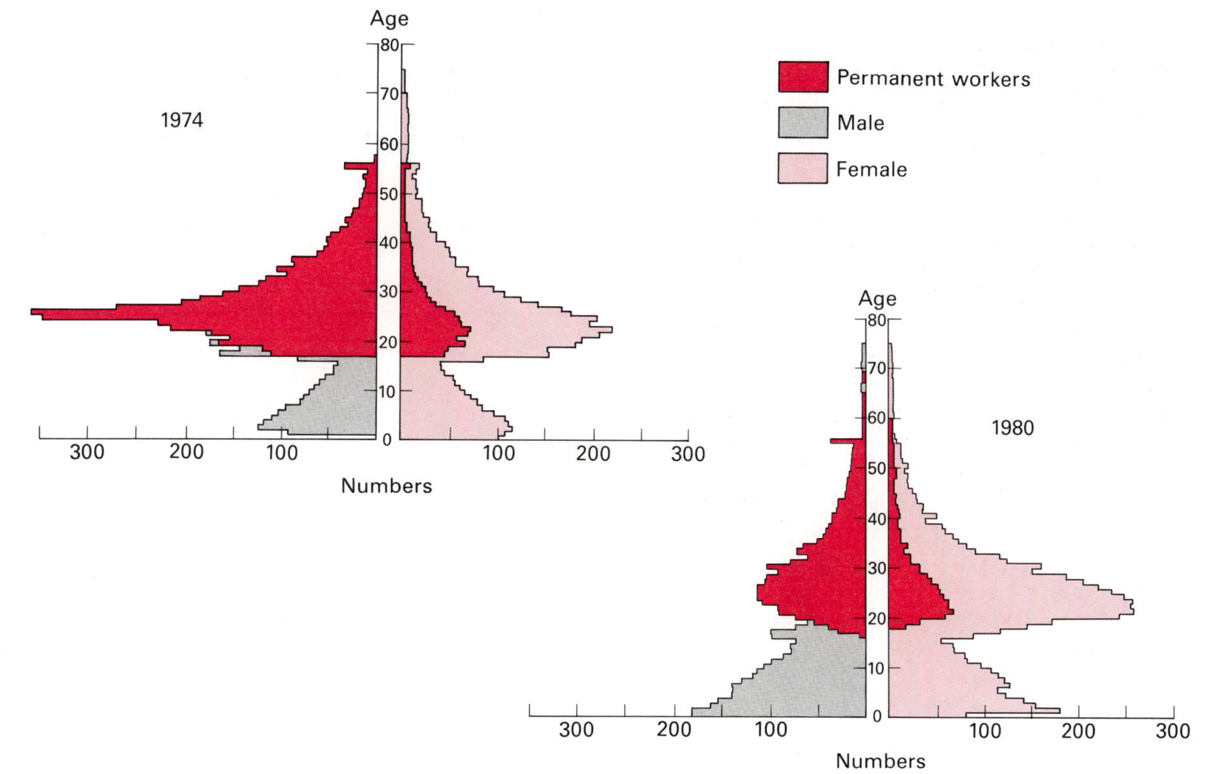

Figure 19.11 Age and sex structure of immigrant workers in France 1974 and 1980.

Table 19.2 Migrant workers to West Germany

Country of origin	1974	1982
Austria	7400	5600
Greece	1800	300
Spain	1200	700
Switzerland	–	500
Turkey	6100	400
Yugoslavia	7700	3300

Table 19.3 Employment of immigrant workers in France, 1979

	% of total employed in each job type
Manufacturing (especially cars)	9.9
Building and Construction	28.0
Commerce (especially catering)	6.0
Transport	6.3
Services (especially medical)	5.7

Coursework ideas

1 Find out where members of your class were born. Show this information as a flow map using arrows to link place of birth to the town or city where you live. Try to explain your map. Find out the reasons why your classmates' families moved. Was it just the result of parents changing jobs?

2 Carry out a survey of migration to Britain. Make up a questionnaire to see what number or percentage of pupils at your school have parents or grandparents who have moved to Britain. Try to discover why they moved. Question at least thirty people so you have a statistically reliable sample.

3 **a** Conduct a survey to find out where members of your form went for their summer holiday. Did most holiday near to home?

b Map the location of where your classmates holidayed.

c What factors influenced the location?

4 a Carry out an investigation to see if peak times for traffic flows reflect the journey-to-work periods. For ten minute periods at 8.30 am; 10.30 am; 12.30 pm; 2.30 pm; 4.30 pm and 6.30 pm on a weekday and on a Saturday or Sunday, count the number and types of vehicles and their direction of travel along a main road between the town centre and your area. Record your information on a tally sheet. Graph the results.

b Make enquiries of local schools and firms of their hours of opening and closing.

i Devise diagrams to show your results.

ii State your conclusions.

Figure 19.12 Nights stayed by overseas and British tourists in the UK in 1988

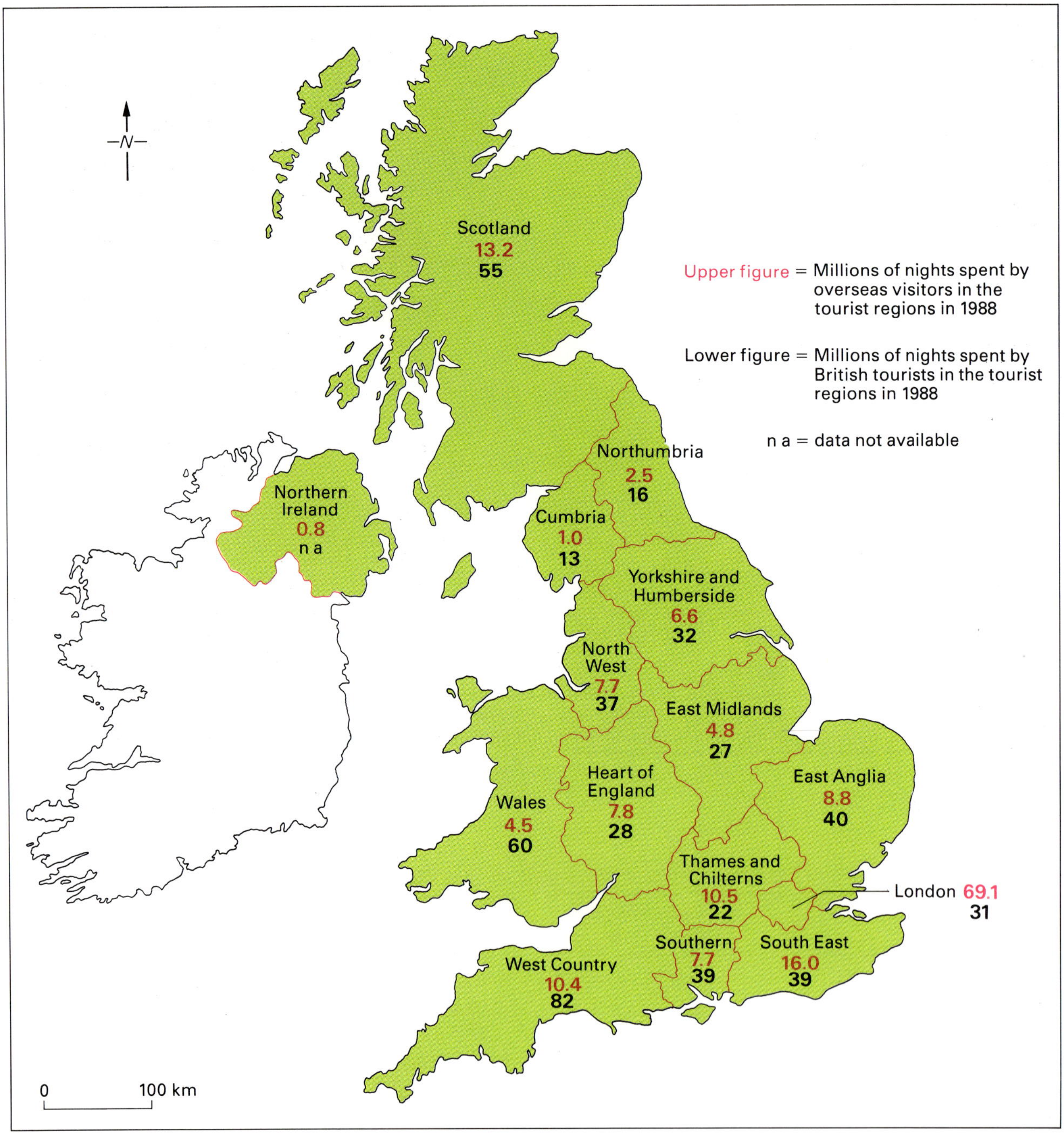

Table 19.4 European visits to and from the United Kingdom in 1978

Country	Number of visits to the UK in thousands	Number of visits to Europe from the UK in thousands
Belgium Luxembourg	740	520
France	1435	2686
West Germany	1507	794
Italy	358	831
Netherlands	1003	571
Denmark	246	106
Republic of Ireland	873	1477
Greece	100	471
Yugoslavia	60	192
Spain	256	2322
Portugal	43	211
Austria	95	199
Switzerland	316	255
Norway	238	101
Sweden	398	73
Finland	55	27
Eastern Europe	83	147

Figure 19.13 Tourists in Italy 1979–1981.

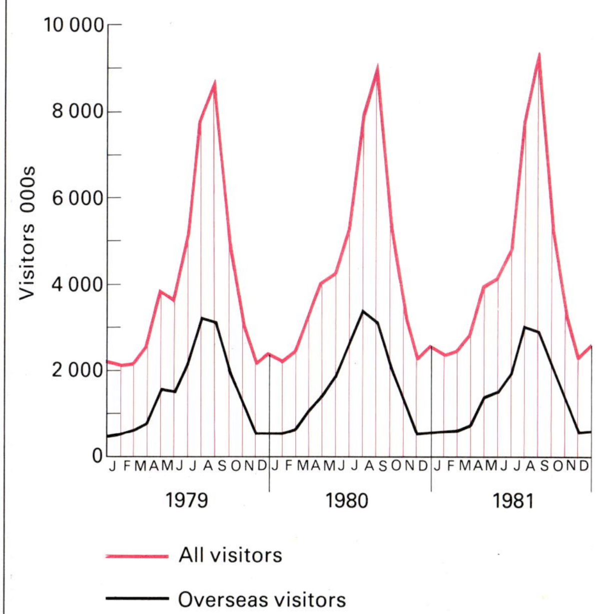

ACTIVITIES

5 a Trace the tourist regions in Britain from Figure 19.12.
   i Shade in one colour the region which accommodated overnight the most overseas visitors in 1988.
   ii Shade in another colour the region which accommodated overnight most British tourists in 1988.
   iii Give the map a title. Make a key.

  b Try to find out reasons for the differences the map reveals.

6 a Using the information in Table 19.4 draw two maps of Europe.
   On one map show the number and countries of origin of tourists to the United Kingdom in 1988
   On the other map show the number and countries of destination of tourists from the United Kingdom in 1988. (Flow lines with the width proportional to the number of holidaymakers will show the information clearly.)

  b Is the number of holidaymakers related to the distance they travel?

7 a From Figure 19.13 describe the peak holiday month in Italy. Use a travel brochure advertising holidays in Italy to find out the location of resorts and what attracts tourists at that time.

  b Make up a poster advertising the attractions of one Italian holiday resort.

8 a Use an atlas map of world air routes to show on a world outline map routes from:
   i London to Barbados;
   ii London to Nairobi, Kenya;
   iii London to the Gambia;
   iv London to Cairo, Egypt;
   v London to Bankok, Thailand.

  b Try to find out from airlines such as British Airways the flight times of these journeys from London.

  c Explain how air travel has reduced the friction of distance between London and the places listed in **a**.

Index